MAY IT ALWAYS BE TRUE

MAY IT ALWAYS BE TRUE

Educating Students in Faith

CHARLES W. POLLARD

Abilene Christian University Press

MAY IT ALWAYS BE TRUE
Educating Students in Faith

ACU
PRESS

Copyright 2011 by Charles W. Pollard

First edition

ISBN 978-0-89112-048-3
LCCN 2010039451

Printed in the United States of America

LIBRARY OF CONGRESS CATALOGING-IN-PUBLICATION DATA
Pollard, Charles W., 1963-
 May it always be true : educating students in faith / Charles Pollard. -- 1st ed.
     p. cm.
 ISBN 978-0-89112-048-3
 1. Christian universities and colleges--Arkansas--Sermons. 2. Sermons, American--21st century. 3. Pollard, Charles W., 1963---Sermons. 4. John Brown University--Presidents--Anecdotes. I. Title.
 BV4310.P65 2010
 252'.55--dc22

                                                                    2010039451

Cover design by Jennette Munger
Interior text design by Sandy Armstrong

Front cover photo: Cathedral of the Ozarks on the campus of John Brown University. Courtesy of John Brown University.

For information contact:
Abilene Christian University Press
1626 Campus Court
Abilene, Texas 79601

1-877-816-4455
www.abilenechristianuniversitypress.com

                     11 12 13 14 15 / 7 6 5 4 3 2

Dedication

For the students of John Brown University.

May following Christ always be true of you.

Contents

CONCLUSION

Acknowledgments

I am deeply grateful to the Board of Trustees at John Brown University who were brave enough to hire a forty-year-old English professor to be their president, then provide time away from the office to complete this book. A supportive board of trustees is a great gift to a university president.

My personal debts are many. Rick Ostrander, Steve Beers, Ed Ericson, Rod Reed, and Tracy Balzer read the introduction and offered keen insights that helped me to strengthen its structure and argument. I have also had the privilege to work with two wise and faithful university chaplains, Stan McKinnon and Rod Reed. Their encouragement and advice have improved my preaching in numerous ways. My cabinet colleagues are generous in their friendship, and their excellence and goodwill makes my job a true joy. The faculty and staff of JBU care deeply for students and have been gracious and kind to Carey and me, and we are honored to work with them. Kory Dale runs the president's office with professionalism and good humor, and I could not even imagine trying to work on this book without her assistance. I also am grateful for the excellent editorial work done by Leonard Allen, Heidi Nobles, and Robyn Leann Burwell at ACU Press. The book is much better because of their scrupulous care.

I want to thank my family. To my parents, Bill and Judy, thank you for your thoughtful comments on these sermons before they were ever delivered and for your love and support throughout my life. To my children: Chad, who encouraged me to "do something" with my chapel talks; Ben, whose questions challenge me to think more deeply and faithfully; Emma, whose quiet belief and keen wit bring a great joy to her father;

and James, whose boundless energy keeps us in the present. And, to my wife, Carey, thank you for your perceptive comments on the book, your generous partnering in the work, and your love, which sustains and sweetens it all.

Finally, I would like to thank the students of JBU. You have been generous in your reception of these words; you have inspired me to deepen my own faith and commitment in your responses. You have challenged me to be transparent in my own struggles and weaknesses in your questions; and you have encouraged me with your hope in the future, your faith in Christ, and your love of others. May it always be true of the students of JBU.

Introduction

About two weeks before my inauguration service at John Brown University, I was walking on campus with my then second-grade son, James. He asked me what I did as president. I was still figuring out all of the different dimensions of the job, so I turned the question around on him and asked him what he thought that I did as president. He paused for a moment and then said: "Well, don't you own all of these buildings, so you must go around and tell people that 'I own this, and I own this, and I own this.'" I laughed and told him that not only did I not own all of these buildings, but that we no longer even owned our home. He was a bit troubled by this revelation of our dependency, but he tried again: "Well, I guess that you go to foreign countries like Texas to talk to people about JBU." We had only lived in Arkansas for two months by that time, but he obviously had already picked up on the regional rivalry and famous independence of Texas. However, when I explained to him that Texas was not a foreign country, he was much less impressed with my visit. Finally, he turned to me and said, "Well, I guess that you spend your time in a lot of boring meetings talking to people. Dad, do you like being the president of JBU?" I assured him that I did on most days, and we headed off to the rugby match.

As I have thought more about my conversation with James, I have wondered if he was not perhaps correct in his description of the job of a university president. While a president may not "own the buildings," he or she does play a critical function in supporting those who carry out the mission of the university, not only in raising funds for facilities, programs, and scholarships, but also in managing the physical infrastructure and educational direction of the university. While Texas may not be a foreign country, a president certainly has a public relations role in representing the university to constituents off-campus, whether they are alumni, parents, investors, community members, government officials, or the news media. And, while every meeting may not be boring, a president's days are often filled with appointments to talk with people about budgets, hiring, curriculum, enrollment, vendors, or programs. I do spend a significant amount of time in development, public relations, strategic planning for the future, and managing resources in the present. The more I thought about it, James was not far off.

However, it is interesting that neither James nor much of contemporary presidential practice expects the university president to be involved directly in educating students, which is the central mission of the university. Before the twentieth century, it would have been a given in both public and private universities that the president had a very public and direct role in the teaching of students. Most colleges and universities would require all seniors to take a capstone class in Moral Philosophy taught by the university president. Moreover, the president, who more often than not was a minister, would also have been expected to address the students regularly in the college chapel. However, as most universities have become larger, more complex, and more overtly secular organizations, the role of the president has gradually moved further and further away from educating students. And, there is some wisdom to this change. As a faculty member said to me, "Lots of us can teach and speak, but often only the president can ask for large gifts, or represent the university to government agencies, or manage the budget process. You should focus on what only the president can do."

This changing role of the president reflects a changing ideal of education in America. As George Marsden and others have shown, while the "American university system was built on the foundation of evangelical Protestant colleges," the process of secularization of American university life has been so thorough and complete that "it has led to the virtual establishment of nonbelief, or the near exclusion of religious perspectives from dominant academic life."[1] Two forces were at play in this transformation. Education was rightly expected to respond to the increasing pluralism in American culture, opening its doors to students and faculty other than white men from established, wealthy, and typically Protestant families. But universities were also expected to meet a public ideal of university education in the same way. By the 1920s, the Protestant establishment in control of the university systems abandoned the distinctive commitments of the evangelical Protestant colleges as too sectarian for this new single educational ideal, but maintained a veneer of the Christian spirit in rhetoric and student life. By the 1960s, the impulse to fulfill a single American educational ideal led logically to the exclusion of any religious belief at all, including mainline Protestant. Secularization became the normative standard for any institution that wanted to be recognized as fulfilling the ideal of American higher education in a pluralistic society.

The role of chapel in university life serves as a convenient marker of this secularization of academic life. Chapel services have played a central role in the life of the university since the Middle Ages, and, as late as 1940, forty-eight percent of schools accredited by the Association of American Universities still had compulsory chapel, twenty percent still had voluntary chapel, and even twenty-seven percent of the state's schools had some form of chapel.[2] However, as most universities, even those founded by churches or denominational boards, have increasingly seen themselves as first and primarily public and secular institutions that fulfill a single, dominant educational ideal, they have had to redefine the missions of their chapel programs to fit within that reality. Often this redefinition seeks to reflect both the Christian history of the institution and the religious neutrality demanded by the secular, pluralist norm. So, for example, on its Web site, Yale University speaks of its chapel program as "supporting and encouraging the expression and vibrancy of a wide array of religious traditions on campus" while at the same time continuing "the strong tradition of Christian worship." Similarly, Duke Chapel delineates Duke's religious position on its Web site: "Duke is not a Christian university, nor does Duke Chapel seek for it to become one. Instead, Duke Chapel would like the University to be known as an institution that values religion (broadly understood) intellectually, culturally and pastorally, that specifically values the contribution of a generous but Trinitarian interdenominational Protestant orthodoxy, expressed through Duke Chapel, and that models how faith traditions can flourish while being experienced and received as a blessing by the culture in which they share." Other universities have more easily adopted religious neutrality as the norm for their chapel program. For example, the Syracuse University Web site describes its Hendricks Chapel as a diverse learning environment that "values differences as a resource for enrichment" and "creatively promotes interfaith understanding and cooperation" by honoring "religious traditions" by encouraging "spiritual introspection" and "active voluntarism." Many faithful Christian faculty, students, and ministries flourish under the pluralist umbrella of these university chapels, a flourishing that we should recognize and commend. However, even though these chapel programs are housed in buildings that still occupy central locations on many campuses, they seem less and less central to defining the identity or educational mission of the university itself.

The mission of John Brown University, in general, and the role of chapel, in particular, certainly has its precedent in the Protestant evangelical college of the nineteenth century, but it also offers a critique of the commonly held ideal for American higher education. At JBU and other similar institutions, Christian commitment is central, not just to the personal life of faculty, staff, and students, but also to the identity of the institution. JBU's mission should not be seen as an attempt to reestablish a Protestant orthodoxy as the general ideal for American education—such a reestablishment is neither wise nor likely given the history of American higher education. JBU's mission does, however, clearly resist secularism as the only available option to define a "true" or "excellent" university that serves the wider public. Moreover, JBU's mission also offers an alternative, institutional response to the pluralism of American life. As Duane Litfin, president of Wheaton College, has argued, "we in Christian higher education . . . believe that a healthy academic marketplace of ideas will view academic freedom as the right not only of individuals but also of voluntary groups or communities of individuals."[3] In other words, true pluralism recognizes the rights, not just of individuals, but of communities of individuals, including educational institutions, to identify themselves in keeping with their religious commitments. So, JBU and other similar institutions stand slightly aslant from the dominant educational ideal and practice.

Personally, I am still drawn to teach and preach as president, in part because it brings me joy, and in part because it enables me to participate directly in the educational mission of the university. I came to the presidency of John Brown University from a faculty position as an English professor at Calvin College and as a former transaction lawyer in an international law firm, Latham & Watkins. While at Calvin I had also served as the board president of a private grammar school as it went through a capital expansion project, so I had some experience with fundraising, construction projects, and board governance. I have attended or worked both at private, Christ-centered institutions (Wheaton, Calvin, and now JBU), and at larger, secular institutions (Harvard Law School, Oxford University, and University of Virginia). Indeed, I have always loved learning and have spent the majority of my life in school settings. When I was offered the job as JBU president, it seemed to be a calling that would bring together my academic, legal, business, and management experiences into a single role. It has been that and so much more.

I left the practice of law to teach English literature because I wanted to interact with undergraduates and to consider with them the important questions of life. Who are we? Why are we here? Why is there joy and pain in life? How should I treat others? Is there a God and does it matter? What should I do in this world? That desire to ask these questions remains an animating part of my work life. I still deeply enjoy engaging with students about these questions in the classroom, at the cafeteria table, or in a chapel address. Moreover, as I often suggest to them, most of these questions cannot be answered without some reference to how people's fundamental commitments shape the way they understand and act in this world. For me, those fundamental commitments are shaped by a desire to be, however imperfectly and partially, a follower of Jesus Christ. And that desire is not just a personal, private expression of religious belief; it is also the institutional commitment. John Brown University exists to educate students to honor God and serve others by challenging them to follow Jesus Christ in their thinking, their affections, and their service. We exist to educate "head, heart, and hand." It is a mission that is not limited to college students, so I trust that these chapel reflections have relevancy to all who seek to follow Christ.

Like all universities, we are committed to educating students to know more: more about great literature, whether it be written by Shakespeare, Woolf, or Walcott; more about human anatomy by working with human cadavers and more about weight-bearing loads by building model bridges; more about beauty by studying color and more about their own history by studying cultures of the past; more about people by living together in a residence hall, more about the local community by serving in it, and more about a culture by learning its language. But, as a Christian university, we also believe that all knowledge is from God so that when we learn more of the natural world, art, politics, or people, we are really learning more about God and the world that he created. For a Christian, learning is an act of worship. Clearly this act of worship happens in the classroom and the library and the student center and the faculty office, but it also happens in chapel. In chapel, we come together and learn more about God, his word, and his world, but we also come together to worship God because all knowledge comes from him.

Christians should also be committed to educating the affections. One of the primary functions of chapel is to encourage students to love and worship the triune God. We train the affections by singing together of God's power and honor, by confessing together our dependence, by celebrating together Christ's death and resurrection, by praying together for God's leading, and by hearing together his word and the witness of his followers. Worship shapes what and how we love, and we seek to structure the worship in chapel to train our affections to love God more fully, more intimately, and more humbly. This love is not just a personal relationship with God. As the great commandment reminds us, loving God involves loving the people and world that he has created. Educating the heart involves training the affections to love mercy, seek justice, promote kindness, and to live righteously in our communities, and in God's world, to hate pride, renounce selfishness, resist greed, and to stop the abuse of others and of God's world.

Educating the hand is sometimes described in the narrow terms of training people for a job, but we should speak of educating students to serve others in the breadth of life's experiences. Chapel should not just affirm what we know and shape what we love; it should also challenge us to do what we can for God and others. Knowledge and love find expression in service in all sorts of different ways in chapel. It happens very directly on Sunday nights when we turn over the whole service to students and ask them to plan and lead the chapel service for the university community. It happens when we hold services to commission spring break or summer mission teams. It happens when we ask the students to give to support families working in the dump in Guatemala City or when I conduct a reverse offering and challenge them to use the money given at chapel to bring about the kingdom of God. It happens in the challenge to sit with the lonely in the cafeteria, to be patient with a roommate in the dorm, to respect a boyfriend on Friday night, to visit with prisoners in the local jail on Sunday, or to recycle cardboard.

We are committed to educate head, heart, and hand because we believe that Christ is over all things. And so, for both personal and institutional reasons, I continue to teach and preach as a university president. Both activities are limited because of the other demands of the job, but I typically speak in chapel half a dozen times a year. I begin with a biblical text, and exposition of that text is a central part of my task, but the topics addressed range widely, from gratitude to sexuality, from faith to doubt, from fear of failure to living as an exile. My selection of texts and topics are shaped by the needs of students and the rhythm of the university calendar, and that principle also animates the organization of this collection. The opening of the school year is always filled with expectations and anxiety, so my chapel addresses at the beginning of the year often challenge students to think first about who we should be as community, trying to draw them out of their own individual hopes and fears. Those addresses are collected in the first section of this book. In the next section, I offer the chapel reflections in which I try to answer that question so central to young people at university: Who am I? The third section collects together Advent sermons, a time in the university calendar when we need to turn again to the wonder of the Incarnation amidst the distraction of final projects, portfolio reviews, exams, Christmas concerts, and parties in the residence halls. In the fourth section, I offer a series of sermons on vocation, asking students to turn outward and to begin to imagine what God would have them do in his world. Finally, I offer a series of Baccalaureate reflections, in which I offer fond farewell and final advice about living as a follower of Jesus Christ after university.

The reflections were drafted for university students, but the texts and themes address issues that confront all of us who seek to live out a life of faith. Indeed, I often find that I am preaching as much to myself in midlife as to the students in the beginning of life, and God has clearly used my time of preparation and presentation as means to instruct me in his way. So, chapel is more than just an opportunity for me to participate in the mission of JBU. It is also a source of great spiritual encouragement and growth to me personally. Chapel offers forty-five minutes of quiet refocusing for me twice a week. It reminds me of the point of the fundraising appeal, the staffing decision, the budget struggle, or the public relations speech. It reminds me that the university's mission is not about me, but about educating students to honor God and serve others. It reminds me that I don't do this work alone as I gather with others. It reminds me that I too need to learn more about Christ, to have my affections shaped to his desires, and to be encouraged to serve him by serving others. It is also the place that I am most often moved to tears, sometimes because of the sadness of living in a world broken by sin, but more often because of the joy of living, working, teaching, playing, and worshiping in a community that collectively affirms that Christ is over all. It is a gift for which I am deeply grateful and a gift that I hope to share with you in writing this book. "May it always be true of us at JBU" is the prayer that I use to end nearly every chapel address. It is a reminder to me and others at the university that we should remain faithful to our commitment to Christ. In writing this book, it is my hope that it will encourage others beyond JBU to remain faithful and thus broaden the scope of that prayer.

CHAPTER 1

Opening the Year

Who Are We? Living in Community

I have been in some sort of school for all but eight years of my life; five of those years were before kindergarten and then three of them were when I practiced law exclusively. Not surprisingly, I have always loved the beginning of the school year: the smell of freshly printed textbooks just brimming with new information to be understood and mastered; the joy of reuniting with old friends and meeting new ones; the sense of starting with a clean slate with only possibilities before you. I also enjoy speaking in the opening chapel because of the expectancy in the air. Shouts of recognition and the buzz of conversation fill the Cathedral sanctuary. We can also count on having a full house on that day; students and faculty are drawn to this place to renew relationships interrupted by a summer break and to celebrate the start of the new semester. Speaking in the first chapel of the semester also enables me to suggest the importance of chapel in our collective task of learning about God and his created world in the university context. Worship is where we begin our work, in the recognition that all knowledge comes from God who has created this world.

Of course, there is also a palpable sense of anxiety in the sanctuary, particularly among the freshmen. Will I be able to meet the professor's expectations? Will I get along with the people in my suite? Will I be able to get a job to help pay for all of this? Why does everyone else look like they are having the time of their lives and I am lonely and afraid? Indeed, studies of retention show that the first six weeks of college life are the most important to the long-term success of students. Colleges and universities have to engage students academically, socially, and, in our case, spiritually within those first six weeks to help them overcome their fear of failure and their deep loneliness. One of the best ways to overcome that fear is to name it. In the first reflection, I try to suggest to students that they are not alone in their anxiety, that it will get better in time, and that we should be a community characterized by faith rather than fear. Of course, our fears are not limited to going to college for the first time. The first reflection in this section was also my first as JBU president, and I too was somewhat frightened by the size of the task before me. Becoming a people of faith and not fear takes a lifetime of learning.

The residential aspect of university life offers a unique opportunity for students to live in community, and it is important to point students toward that community as a support system within which they can conquer their anxieties. They come to college and stuff their 200 cubic feet of stuff into their 150 cubic feet of space in the dorm room. They are sharing that intimate living space with another person, often for the first time in their lives and often with a person that they don't know. They are also sharing a bathroom with four or six people in a suite or sometimes twenty-five people on a floor. They have ready access to a host of activities with their peers, including intramural sports, retreats, service projects, ministries, and theater and music opportunities. Conversations from class spill over to discussions in the student center. The faculty member who helps you in the laboratory may sit next to you in the cafeteria. The supervisor of your work-study job may greet you in church on Sunday. The intensity of residential higher education experience offers wonderful opportunities for young people to learn how best to contribute to, and benefit from, others in a community. Many of those lessons are learned through the programming in the residence halls and through the culture transmitted by the faculty and staff. However, chapel also provides the opportunity to encourage students to see and to shape the collective identity of our community.

The next three chapel addresses fall into that category. In the first, I explore Luke's rendition of Christ's healing of the ten lepers to suggest that a community can be characterized by gratitude only when its members recognize how dependent they are on others to meet our most basic needs. In the second, I use Ernest Gordon's *To End All Wars*, which was our summer reading selection one year, as my primary illustration to explain what a community characterized by the great commandment might look like. Gordon was the former chaplain of Princeton University, and his memoir records his experience in a Japanese prison camp during World War II. He shows how the prisoners remained humane in the camp by showing kindness to one another, both in word and in deed, both by setting up what was essentially a liberal arts college in the jungle and by feeding the hungry and taking care of the sick. The final sermon in this section was offered at a community worship service that was held in the university's gymnasium for students and for members of the local churches. The ministerial alliance organized the event and asked me to preach. I agreed, in part, to have a chance to think through unity in church, a unity reflected in the university's interdenominational identity. We have over forty different denominations represented among our students, and our faculty and staff attend around twenty-five to thirty different churches. The community holds together, not by an easy ecumenicalism, but by conscientious practicing of that time-honored, interdenominational principle: "in essentials, unity; in non-essentials, liberty; and in all things, charity." It is a principle that is good for students to learn as they develop their own spiritual resiliency, and as they come to define their own core faith convictions and imagine becoming a part of different local churches in the future.

Faith, gratitude, kindness, and unity should characterize our communities beyond the walls of the university, and I hope that these reflections will encourage others to implement these lessons of living in community in their own churches, neighborhoods, and workplaces.

Be a People of Faith, Not of Fear

Text: Matthew 14:22-33

Immediately Jesus made the disciples get into the boat and go on ahead of him to the other side, while he dismissed the crowd. After he had dismissed them, he went up on a mountainside by himself to pray. When evening came, he was there alone, but the boat was already a considerable distance from land, buffeted by the waves because the wind was against it.

During the fourth watch of the night Jesus went out to them, walking on the lake. When the disciples saw him walking on the lake, they were terrified. "It's a ghost," they said, and cried out in fear.

But Jesus immediately said to them. "Take courage. It is I. Don't be afraid."

"Lord, if it's you," Peter replied, "tell me to come to you on the water."

"Come," he said.

Then Peter got down out of the boat and walked on the water to Jesus. But when he saw the wind, he was afraid and, beginning to sink, cried out, "Lord, save me!"

Immediately Jesus reached out his hand and caught him. "You of little faith," he said, "why did you doubt?"

And when they climbed into the boat, the wind died down. Then those who were in the boat worshiped him, saying, "Truly you are the Son of God."

I would like to begin today with a confession. Now don't get too excited. It is not some secret problem that the presidential search committee was unable to unearth. It is simply one of my fears. I am afraid of heights, a fear that manifests itself in very specific ways. For instance, I had no problem working on the fifty-eighth floor of the Sears Tower, or looking out the window of an airplane, or strapped into a rollercoaster. I only experience this cold, irrational, heart-clutching, palm-sweating fear when I am a couple of stories up and in an open-air space. For example, when I first saw the Alpine Tower on the experiential learning challenge course on campus, my pulse began to race as I irrationally imagined climbing it without a safety harness. This fear takes on two forms for me. First, it is a personal fear; when I climb to a high place and look out into the middle distance, I have this fear that I will have an uncontrollable impulse to jump. Second, this fear is even more acute and irrational when I am with my children. Whenever we are together as a family at a place of great height, I start to imagine my kids stumbling over the edge of a mountain cliff or falling through a gap in a restraining fence and tumbling hundreds of feet to their deaths. I know that it is a completely irrational fear, but that knowledge does not prevent me from breaking out in a sweat when I am in high places.

Now typically my fear of heights is easy to deal with it. I work on the second floor of the Chapman Administration building, I live in a ranch-style house, and I avoid things like Alpine Towers on challenge courses. However, a few years ago, my family and I lived in England for about five months. I was directing a semester abroad program for Calvin College, and part of my duties included planning a variety of excursions for the students and several side trips for my family. The problem, of course, with these trips was that they often involved climbing old castles and cathedrals as well as steep hills and mountains, most of which were more than two-stories high and none of which were fully enclosed by glass. Even worse, my kids seem to think that these ancient monuments and majestic cliffs were actually playgrounds, and they proceed to jump, run, swing, and lean as if the rules of gravity and death did not apply to them. Two examples should suffice.

We went to Salisbury Cathedral, which is famous because it was built in the thirteenth century on a swamp and its spire towers some four hundred feet in the air and leans noticeably. In fact, architects and engineers have wondered how the tower has remained standing. So what do the church wardens of Salisbury Cathedral decide to do in all their wisdom: they offer one and a half hour tours of this leaning tower to tourists. The tour begins by looking at one of the four main pillars of the cathedral, a pillar that is noticeably bent from the weight of the tower. Then, you walk up a winding stair case to a point just under the cathedral ceiling and look down about one hundred or so feet while the guide tells you about how many workmen fell to their death in building the cathedral. Then you walk up a wooden staircase within the tower while the guide points out all of the different ways in which architects and engineers have sought to secure the tower: from the early wooden scaffolding to metal bands wrapped around support pillars, to a complex series of crisscrossing wires that literally hold the tower together. Finally, when you reach about two-thirds of the way up, they take you "outside" of the tower for another panoramic view and the only thing between you and certain death is a crumbling, seven-hundred-year-old wall. I was noticeably shaking by the time I got back down.

Toward the end of the trip, my family and I went to the Lake District in the north part of England. It is beautiful countryside with large, grass-covered hills, almost small mountains, which the English call fells, and "fell-walking" is one of the suggested activities. Now my kids have a name for when their parents plan an activity for the whole family; they call it FFF—Forced Family Fun. And they had considered the entire five months in England to be one long FFF. However, I thought that walking along the fell would be an adventure, and it looked completely safe from our hotel window. So we set out midmorning and began our trek up Coniston Fell. However, much to my horror, what had looked like a relatively easy slope and wide trail turned out to be an incredibly steep and narrow sheep path. As we got closer to the summit, the path became so narrow and steep that we were actually scrambling up the rocks on hand and knees. After about two hours of hiking, we got within about five hundred yards of the summit and I looked up. I saw a narrow, single-file path with what looked to me like sheer cliffs on either side. I then looked down at my beautiful family and told them I didn't think it was worth the risk of going all the way up. Instead of grateful respect for their father's wise guidance, I received hoots, scorn, and anger. "You can't mean to tell us that you are going to take us on this FFF walk for two hours and then not let us go to the top," my affectionate sixteen-year-old son, Chad, said. Even my beloved wife of twenty years questioned me. I told them I just couldn't help it and I sat on the mountain clutching the hillside. My wife Carey finally convinced me to allow her and Chad to go to the top.

As you can see, I have thought a lot about my fear of heights. The corollary of my fear is a lack of faith. I don't trust that the safety railing put in place at a castle will hold the weight of my eleven-year-old girl. I don't trust that Salisbury spire, which has stood for some seven hundred years, will stand another day. I don't trust that my otherwise coordinated children will be able to walk up a path that hundreds of people walk up every week. I fear because I do not have confidence in the ordinary things of life.

While I can manage my fear of heights by staying close to the ground in my second-floor office and in my ranch-style house, managing our fear by avoiding it is not always what God calls us to do. Let us turn again to the Scripture to see how we might respond to our fears.

"The winds were against them."

Notice first that Christ makes the disciples go ahead without him. As the King James Version translates it, Christ "constrained his disciples to get into the boat." And, once they were out into the lake, the winds went against them, or the "wind was contrary." Metaphorically, we know that there will be times in our lives when we feel alone and when the winds of life are contrary and buffeting us. It may be your parents telling you that they no longer love each other and have decided to separate. It may be the doctors telling your grandfather that they have seen a spot on his x-ray and that they will need to do a biopsy. It may be the loss of a job or the relocating of a family. The contrary winds of life come in many manifestations. They can also be the challenge of organic chemistry, the difficulty of a roommate, the impending deadline for a paper, or the overwhelming sense of sadness from depression. Indeed, these contrary winds may actually come from experiences that we seek out, experiences such as choosing to attend college or to take on the job of president. When the winds of life are buffeting us, we are often afraid.

Notice that the disciples are so afraid that they do not even recognize Christ when he comes to them: "When the disciples saw him walking on the lake, they were terrified. 'It's a ghost,' they said, and cried out in fear." They are so caught up in the storm that they see a ghost rather than Christ, a figure that will increase their terror rather than a person who might bring help. It is understandable, perhaps, because the disciples had little experience with a person walking on the water. However, these are the same disciples who just saw Jesus heal the sick and feed five thousand with five loaves and two fishes. When the winds of life are against us, let us not be too quick to see a ghost whom we can blame instead of the Christ who brings help.

"Take courage. It is I. Don't be afraid."

Christ then offers what I think are three of the most encouraging short sentences in Scripture. "Take courage. It is I. Don't be afraid." Let us take each phrase in its turn.

"Take courage," which can also be interpreted as "have confidence" or "be of good cheer." It is a command of Christ, not a recommendation. When the winds of life are against us, we should have confidence and courage. And what is courage? Courage is moving to college without

29

knowing a soul; it is walking into the hospital room of a dying person; it is taking the course that will stretch you but may hurt your GPA; it is loving again after you have been hurt in a relationship; it is having confidence even in the face of the buffeting winds, confidence not in your own success or in the absence of struggle, but confidence in the person of Jesus Christ.

Second, "It is I." We must recognize the source of our confidence is Christ. The Greek construction of the passage emphasizes this point by repeating the pronoun "I." It could be translated, albeit an awkward construction in English, "I I am," with perhaps a faint echo of God's claim that "I am that I am." Our source of confidence has to be in the person of Christ, not in our own achievements or abilities to control the situation. We have confidence in Christ, not because he ensures us success, but because he is who he is. He does not promise that we won't feel the sting of the buffeting winds. We know that Christian marriages break apart, that people of faith die of cancer, that you may take organic chemistry and fail, that your offering of friendship may be rejected, that your article may not be accepted, that your fundraising request may be denied. However, we have confidence because we know to whom we belong, that the source of our value and worth is in our relationship to Christ, not in our degrees, successes, achievements, beauty, possessions, grades, or affirmation of others. We have confidence, in other words, not in our ability to row against the wind, but in Christ's power to control the wind if he chooses.

Third, "Don't be afraid." The corollary to confidence is not being afraid, and it is the command that is repeated more than any other in Scripture. Christ is continually telling his disciples and us: "Don't be afraid." "Don't be afraid." "Don't be afraid." It is the command that we should tell each other every day: "don't be afraid" as you apply for that internship; "don't be afraid" as you tutor that child; "don't be afraid" to love that person who seems unlovable. Fear is the opposite of faith. Christ's command not to be afraid does not, of course, guarantee success.

It is not "don't be afraid" because everything will be solved, but don't be afraid because Christ is who he is. He is in control, not us. He is the one who defines success and failure. He is the one running this show.

"Lord, if it's you," Peter said, "tell me to come to you on the water."

Now, as far as I am concerned, the story could have ended there with those three, short phrases of encouragement. But it does not. And, in many ways, Peter's example reinforces with miraculous specificity and humanity the general point that Christ has already made with all of the disciples: have confidence; it is me; don't be afraid.

Peter asks the challenging question: "Lord, if it's you, tell me to come to you on the water." It is one of the times in Scripture when I wish that we had a soundtrack to hear the inflection of Peter's voice. Is he asking boldly, foolishly, curiously, skeptically, or bluntly? Is he testing Jesus or is he just longing to be with him? Whatever the inflection of Peter's question, Christ answers with the word that we all long to hear when we face a time of struggle. He simply tells Peter to "come."

Come, Peter, in the midst of the storm and be with me. Come, Peter, and recognize that I can do more than you could ever imagine in this time of struggle if you will have confidence in me. Come, Peter, and walk on water in the midst of these buffeting winds. It is the same message that we should hear: Come and let me be your parents as your parents fight. Come and let me be your health as you face the uncertainty of illness. Come and let me love you when you have faced rejection. Come and let me be your success as you experience the disappointment of failure. Come. Come. Come.

"Then Peter got down out of the boat and walked on the water to Jesus."

And Peter, bless his heart, gets out of the boat and begins to walk toward Jesus. Whether he was testing Jesus or not, he does take that step and becomes an example of courage for us all. He does not remain in the relative safety of the boat with the other disciples, the safety of what is known, the safety of being with the group; instead, he overcomes his fear and steps out alone to walk to Christ.

Peter also, bless his heart, fails. His focus turns from the person to the problem, from Christ to the storm ("he saw the wind"), and he begins to sink and has to cry out, "Lord, save me!" And Christ is ever full of mercy. Notice what the text says: Christ "immediately" reaches out his hand and catches him. Christ does not play with Peter. He does not let him flounder awhile in order to teach Peter a lesson about his doubt. He immediately reaches out his hand and catches him up. He does say the hard word to Peter ("You of little faith, why did you doubt?"), but again it would be interesting to hear the sound track. Is it a word of hard condemnation or affectionate recognition of Peter's weakness? Christ sustains Peter even though he has little faith.

If you are like me, you would have been with the rest of the disciples in the boat. You and I might agree with the general proposition that we should be people of faith and not of fear, but that does not mean we are going to do something foolish like actually step out of the boat into the storm. But should we be so cautious? Should we be huddled in the boat, intellectually affirming Christ's claim of faith over fear, or should we step out of the boat and be in the midst of the storm looking to come to Christ? We should not overly romanticize this step out of the boat. The likelihood is that we will fail, that we will begin to sink in the storm, that we will not have the faith necessary to stay upright, and that we will have to cry out to Jesus to be saved once again. But, you know what? He will respond. The same Christ who tells us to "Come" is the same Christ who reaches out his hand "immediately" to save us when we begin to sink. So how could we become people characterized by faith not by fear? What would it look like? Let me posit a few tentative characteristics:

- We would be characterized as a people who spend their time looking for Christ in the storm, not blaming the ghost for it.
- We would be a people of confidence, not the brash and arrogant confidence of knowing all the right answers to life's questions, but the quiet confidence of a people who know to whom they belong.
- We would be a people who are not threatened by the ideas of others because we are confident in the truth of Christ.
- We would be a people less focused on controlling our world and more focused on being controlled by God.
- We would be a people who are willing to step out of the boat and be in the midst of the storm. We would not shrink away from the hurt that is a part of living in this world, but we would not be overwhelmed by it. We would be willing to take risks because success and failure are not defined or controlled by our efforts.

As Jesus says in John 16:33, "I have told you these things, so that in me you may have peace. In this world you will have trouble. But take heart [same word, have confidence or faith], I have overcome the world." If Christ has already overcome the world, then perhaps we need not worry so much about overcoming it ourselves; instead we should enter the storm and allow God to use us to transform the world to conform it to his likeness.

We should be a people of faith, not of fear, because we have heard the end of the story. As novelist Frederick Buechner says, "The worst isn't the last thing about the world. It's the next to the last thing."[1] We can have confidence, faith, to live out our lives for Christ because we know that the last thing is the best thing, and that last and best thing is Christ.

And notice how the passage ends: "Then those who were in the boat worshiped him, saying, 'Truly you are the Son of God.'" People who are characterized by faith and not by fear recognize Christ as the Son of God and they worship him.

May it always be true of us.

"Unclean, Unclean": Recognizing Need and Responding with Gratitude

Text: Luke 17:11-19

Now on his way to Jerusalem, Jesus traveled along the border between Samaria and Galilee. As he was going into a village, ten men who had leprosy met him. They stood at a distance and called out in a loud voice, "Jesus, Master, have pity on us!"

When he saw them, he said, "Go, show yourselves to the priests." And as they went, they were cleansed.

One of them, when he saw he was healed, came back, praising God in a loud voice. He threw himself at Jesus' feet and thanked him—and he was a Samaritan.

Jesus asked, "Were not all ten cleansed? Where are the other nine? Was no one found to return and give praise to God except this foreigner?" Then he said to him, "Rise and go; your faith has made you well."

To understand this gospel story, you first have to understand the nature of leprosy in biblical times. The biblical term leprosy covers much more than what we now consider to be leprosy. In our modern use, leprosy is the common name for Hansen's disease, a disease of the skin which kills the nerve endings and which often leads to blotchy skin ulcers and to the deforming or loss of extremities like fingers and toes. At its worst, Hansen's disease can have horrible disfiguring effects on the entire body, including the face. In the Bible, the term leprosy likely included Hansen's disease but it was also much broader, covering many infectious skin diseases.

We do know that leprosy in biblical times carried a great social stigma with it. The early Israelites knew enough about infectious skin diseases to know that they were contagious, and they responded by isolating the people with the disease. Leviticus 13 summarizes the Old Testament teaching on skin diseases, and it ends with this command: "The person with such an infectious disease must wear torn clothes, let his hair be unkempt, cover the lower part of his face and cry out, 'Unclean! Unclean!' As long as he has the infection he remains unclean. He must live alone; he must live outside the camp" (Lev. 13:45-46). In latter rabbinic teaching, the law required lepers to maintain space of six feet between themselves and healthy people. In medieval times, lepers were forced to carry bells or clappers to announce their presence, and they often were required to attend their own funeral mass before they were excommunicated from the community. It is also not just in Western or biblical communities that lepers were shunned. In the Far East, leprosy was considered punishment for sexual immorality; in India, it was a punishment for an offense committed by a person in an earlier life; in Africa, it was evidence of the spirits' displeasure.

Consider the plight of lepers throughout history: not only do they have a crippling disease that likely causes pain and suffering, but they must also leave their home and family, live outside the village often in caves or shacks, beg for food because they can't work, and then publicly announce their sickness in dress and speech—"unclean, unclean." Once they were diagnosed, all that they could expect from others was fear and scorn. In short, people who had leprosy were not just sick, they were ritually unclean. They were excommunicated from the community; they were untouchable; they were to be alone.

People do not contract leprosy because of a volitional choice, but because we live in a fallen, sinful world in which disease inflicts damage. However, imagine what it would be like if we all had to announce our own particular manifestation of living in a sinful world. Imagine people walking through the university in torn rags with unkempt hair, shouting: "unclean, unclean: I am a gossip"; "unclean, unclean: I love money and consume irresponsibly"; "unclean, unclean: I can't control my sexual desires"; "unclean, unclean: I don't care about the poor"; or "unclean, unclean: I hate my roommate." Sin permeates our world. Whether it is manifested in diseases or disasters or in the individual choices that we make to be selfish or evil, sin permeates our world. We are all unclean and that sin isolates us from each other even if we do not publicly announce it.

"Jesus, Master, have pity on us."

However, Christ responds when we call out for mercy in our sinful condition. The ten lepers see him approach, and they cry out for pity. We are not sure about the level of their expectations when they make this plea. It was a common practice for lepers to place themselves at the road into the village so that they could beg for food or money. They were the equivalent of the homeless person who makes his way to the bus stop or the train station to ask for some change: "Jesus, Master, can you spare a dollar for food?" Perhaps, however, these ten lepers had heard of Christ's reputation and were hoping for more. Perhaps they had heard of this Christ who had broken the Levitical laws and actually touched a leper and healed him as it is recorded in Luke 5. Perhaps they just knew of his reputation for healing, and they were hoping to be restored to health and to the community.

"Go, show yourself to the priests."

They cry out, and Christ responds, but his response is different from his earlier healing in Luke 5. He does not touch these lepers; instead, he commands them: "Go, show yourself to the priests." This command was in keeping with the ritual laws of Judaism because only the priest could declare that someone was cleansed of leprosy—cleansed in the sense of healed from the disease, but also cleansed in the sense of being ritually brought back into the community. Notice, however, that these ten lepers are not cleansed by Christ's command: they are not instantly cleansed when he speaks, but only when they begin to obey his command. The Scripture says, "And as they went, they were cleansed." It was not until they took action in obedience to Christ's word that they began to see the results. Christ often points us in a new direction and expects us to obey before we are sure of the results. It might be the decision to come to the university even though you are not sure you can make it financially. Or it might be the decision to break a bad habit by seeing a counselor even though you have been involved in this habit for years. It might be the decision to move to a new part of the country after graduation because of the calling of a new job. It might be the decision to move closer to family to take care of an elderly parent even though you are giving up the relationships in your church and community. Many of the decisions in our lives involve a discerning of God's will and obedience to that discernment, with no assurance of the results. Instead, Christ calls us to obey and trust him for the results.

"He threw himself at Jesus' feet and thanked him—and he was a Samaritan."

This gospel story could have ended here as another example of Christ's healing ministry. However, Scripture goes on to record a second part to the story, the story of the grateful Samaritan. The fact that he was a Samaritan raises several interesting issues. Samaritans were a mixed people, both in their ethnicity and their religious practices. They had been Israelites but were almost overwhelmed by intermarriage with other groups, and they had adopted many of the non-Jewish practices of these other people. The Jews scorned the Samaritans for the impurity of their blood and their worship. So, this Samaritan was doubly scorned, first because he was a Samaritan and second because he was a leper.

However, he is the only one who comes back to thank Christ and praise God for his healing. Why? Well you can imagine that the other nine went to the priest and then immediately went to their families to celebrate. They had been restored to health, but they had also been restored to the community. They were no longer social outcasts. Perhaps for the first time in many years, they could kiss their spouses, embrace their parents, shake hands with their neighbors, and pick up their kids. They could even begin to plan for a future that included work, family, friends, and synagogue—a normal life. They had almost literally been brought back from the dead to join the living. Even if you cannot excuse them, you can imagine how they might forget to thank Christ in all of the jubilation.

Ten had faith to follow Christ's command, and they were cleansed. Only one, however, also had gratitude, and he is healed and made whole. The passage clearly draws the distinction between the Jewish lepers and the Samaritan to the detriment of the Jews. As the Scripture says, "One of them, when he saw he was healed, came back, praising God in a loud voice. He threw himself at Jesus' feet and thanked him—and he was a Samaritan. Jesus asked, 'Were not all ten cleansed? Where are the other nine? Was no one found to return and give praise to God except this foreigner?'"

It is the Samaritan, the one whom the Jews would look down upon as the heathen, the half-breed, the outsider. He is the only one who returns to thank Jesus and praise God. Why? Perhaps the Samaritan was more ready to thank Christ because he came from a greater place of need. He knew that he was still a Samaritan, thus he remained a social outcast and so was more intensely grateful for the healing that he did receive. Moreover, Scripture seems to suggest that recognizing our need is a prerequisite to living right. When Scripture makes a distinction between the Jews and the Samaritans, between Pharisees and the tax collectors, or between the self-righteous believers and the needy sinners, it almost invariably favors the person who recognizes the personal need for help. I have to tell you that these distinctions make me uncomfortable because I am probably much closer to the Jewish lepers than to the grateful Samaritan, much closer to the Pharisee then to the needy sinner. I don't want to admit that I am needy in my professional life, in my family life, in my spiritual life; I don't want to admit that I am unclean. I want to be successful and in control. I want to do things for God, not have him do things for me. I want to be thanked for the things that I do rather than thanking others for the things that they do for me.

It is only the Samaritan who fully recognizes the extent of his need and who returns to Christ with thanks and praise and worship. Christ responds, "Rise and go; your faith has made you well." Christ is full of grace; he does not strike down the nine with leprosy again. However, it is the grateful Samaritan who is not only cleansed but also made well—made whole.

Gratitude comes from recognizing our need, recognizing that we can't do it ourselves, that we are unclean and alone, that we desperately require help. Moreover, gratitude is by its very nature a form of praise to God. The word used for thanks, "*eucharist*," is, of course, the same word that some Christian traditions use to describe communion, one of our central acts of thanks and worship. When we thank someone for their help, we recognize our insufficiency and our dependence on God. We engage in an act of worship. God primarily works through other people to achieve his ends. He puts us into relationships with other people so that they can meet our deepest needs—our needs for acceptance, food, clothing, good work, forgiveness, education, beauty, friendship, love— and we don't thank those other people nearly enough.

If I have learned anything in my role as president, I have learned that I can't do it alone. Not only am I not omniscient and omnipresent, but I am also needy and unclean. However, God almost never asks us to do things all alone. He provides us with other people who compensate for our weaknesses, who extend words of encouragement, who engage in work that we are unable to do, who offer the grace of forgiveness even when we are unclean, who meet our deepest needs, who touch us with the love of God. Our response should be one of gratitude for these people because they are often the means by which God meets our need for healing and restores us to community. And, as the Gospel suggests, when we thank them, we should also offer praise to God for putting these people in our lives.

So, if you would indulge me a moment, I need to thank a few people for the ways in which they have extended God's grace to me this past summer. I want to thank Fred from facility services, who took apart our kitchen plumbing to remove a dish rag that had clogged the disposal—a clog that occurred in our university house the night before we left on vacation—because I need help when it comes to plumbing. I want to thank Davin and Josh, both digital media students who worked over the weekend to help me finish my presentations, because I need help when it comes to digital media. I want to thank Professor Siemans for asking good questions in our faculty meetings because I need to hear from an audience to know whether I make myself clear. I want to thank Robbie who stopped by my office this summer just to say hello and to tell me about his work at camp because I need to hear from students when it gets quiet and lonely around here in the summertime. And, before this begins to sound like an Oscar acceptance speech, I want to thank Carey for talking with me, going on walks, encouraging me to get away, holding my hand, because I have a deep need for friendship and she is my best friend. Most of all, I want to thank and praise God for placing me in this community of believers.

I also know that I cannot do this gratitude thing by myself. We need to become a community characterized by gratitude, a place in which a thank you is as common as a greeting, but we must first become a community in which we are willing to recognize that we are needy. So I challenge you to examine your life and recognize your needs, and then see who God has placed in your life to meet that need and thank them. Thank them with a note or an email, a text message, a flower, a hug, a rugby tackle, a telephone call, a high five, or whatever way you find appropriate. And then praise God for the ways he extends his grace to you through other people. For you see, the shape of this narrative in Luke—a story in which a person recognizes himself as unclean, begs for mercy, follows Christ's command, is healed, and returns to thank and praise God—is the shape of the gospel. It is the good news of salvation, and it should be the shape of the story of our lives.

May it always be true of us.

Kindness: The University as Prison Camp

Text: Mark 12:28-31

One of the teachers of the law came and heard them debating. Noticing that Jesus had given them a good answer, he asked him. "Of all the commandments, which is the most important?"

"The most important one," answered Jesus, "is this: 'Hear, O Israel, the Lord our God, the Lord is one. Love the Lord your God with all your heart and with all your soul and with all your mind and with all your strength." The second is this: "Love your neighbor as yourself." There is no commandment greater than these.

What do you think of feet? What do you think about touching someone else's feet? My children consider feet to be perhaps the ugliest and most unseemly part of the body, and they are convinced that you should never touch someone else's feet. It is no surprise then that my children object loud and long when I rub Carey's feet, or, which happens more often and much to my happiness, when Carey will rub my feet. After a long day at work, I find myself on the couch watching a ballgame or the news, and Carey will come into the room and offer to rub my feet and then the kids start running for the doors. This foot-rubbing is purely platonic—it is not leading to something else—but it is deeply relaxing and refreshing. Similarly, I will often be the first to wake up in the morning and bring her a cup of coffee in bed. I know that she enjoys waking up to the smell of coffee, and the first few sips help her move from the world of sleep to the world of life, a transition that she sometimes finds difficult. It is a joy to see the sleepy smile on her face when I set the coffee down on the bedside table.

Okay, by now perhaps you are wondering to yourself, why is the president telling us these things? You are perhaps, like my kids, looking for a way to head for the doors. This foot-rubbing and coffee-bringing business is just way too much information. I would like to suggest that foot-rubbing and coffee-bringing are ordinary acts of kindness, and that ordinary acts of kindness may be at the heart of the Great Commandment. Let me explain by returning again to the Scripture.

Now first we should understand the context for this passage. Christ has already made his triumphant entry into Jerusalem, and Good Friday and Easter are looming ahead at the end of the week. The chief priests, teachers of the law, and the elders have spent the better part of the week asking Jesus questions to "catch him in his words." They have asked him questions about his authority, about whether they should pay taxes to Caesar, about who will be married to whom in the resurrection. This question, however, is different from those "gotcha" questions because this teacher of the law is genuinely curious about Christ's response. This question was a question that had been debated for many centuries in the Jewish tradition. What is the most important commandment? An alternative way to ask this question in Jewish culture would be to ask someone to "teach me the whole Torah while standing on one foot." To meet that challenge, you have to summarize concisely, speak quickly, and have good balance.

In one sense, Christ's response is not that remarkable and certainly not that creative. He merely recites two well-known Old Testament Scriptures. First, he quotes Deuteronomy 6:4-5: "Hear, O Israel: the Lord our God, the Lord is one. Love the Lord your God with all your heart and with all your soul and with all your strength." Christ does revise the list in Deuteronomy by adding a fourth element, loving God with all of your mind, but he still clearly is echoing the *Shema*, for this is the first verse of the collection of Scriptures that pious Jews would repeat every morning and evening as a confession of faith. Second, Christ quotes from the second part of Leviticus 19:18: "Do not seek revenge or bear a grudge against one of your people, but love your neighbor as yourself." Indeed, even putting these two commandments together is not completely new; other Jewish thinkers had asserted that the love of God and the love of neighbor were complementary truths. What is striking, of course, about Christ's response is the authority from which he speaks. When he summarizes the law, he speaks with the authority of the one who has come to fulfill the law. To understand this authority, let us look at three of the central ideas in this passage.

"Hear, O Israel, the Lord our God, the Lord is one."

Christ begins with God and his character. The first command is to listen, accept, and obey that the Lord our God, the Lord is one. In other words, our faith begins in acknowledgment that God is God, which is also an acknowledgment , or perhaps more accurately, a confession, that we are not God. We are not in charge of our world, our friends, our family, our careers, or even of our own lives. We are not necessary or sufficient. We have no purpose, or meaning, or even being without God. It is always a good reminder to begin with God and to say to one another: "Hear, O JBU, the Lord our God, the Lord is one."

"Love the Lord your God with all your heart and with all your soul and with all your mind and with all your strength."

After hearing and accepting that the Lord is God, Christ commands us to love God with all our heart and with all our soul and with all our mind and with all our strength. These attributes are overlapping and reinforcing. For instance, in Jewish thought, the heart is the seat of the spiritual life and the inner being, but it also conveys the sense of the mind and understanding. Similarly the soul refers to life itself and incorporates our feelings, emotions, and desires, and so overlaps in meaning with heart. Mind refers to the intelligence and reasoning, and strength reflects

45

one's ability, will, capacity, and power to act. This list encompasses our entire being. We should love the Lord our God with all aspects of our being. Our love for God should move us emotionally. Our love for God should tax us intellectually. Our love for God should stretch us physically. Our love for God should shape our spiritual character. Our love of God should define the inner core of our personality. There is no part of our being that should not respond to God's character.

Moreover, to love God with all of your heart, all of your soul, all of your mind, and all of your strength means being willing to surrender all your heart, all your soul, all your mind, and all your strength to his calling. God is calling us to conform our innermost being to his image. Disciplining ourselves to read Scripture and to pray regularly is a way to love God. We should obey. God is calling us to direct our emotions and passions in a way that honors him. Controlling our anger and encouraging friendship are ways to love God. We should obey. God is calling us to use our minds to understand the intricacies of his creation, of his people, of his histories, of his cultures. Doing our homework is a way to love God. We should obey. God is calling us to exert our talents and skills to their utmost to bring about beauty and to serve others. Running with reckless abandon on the soccer field, creating a poem, dissecting a cadaver, or tutoring a grade-school child are all ways to love God. We should obey. The Lord our God, the Lord is one and when he commands us to love him, he commands us to love him with our whole life. We should obey.

"Love your neighbor as yourself."

Loving God is inextricably linked to loving your neighbor. They are complementary truths. The Great Commandment begins with God and an understanding of him, it then moves to obeying God by loving him with our whole being, and it concludes by loving those who have been made in God's image, by loving our neighbors. Ah, but there is the rub.

It is one thing to say that we will love God. It is another thing to say that we will love our roommate, our sibling, or the colleague in our department. God is God, and we can submit ourselves to him, but it is much more difficult to submit ourselves to other human beings, to have their interests be more important than our own. Indeed, it is often easier to love the person who is halfway around the world than it is to love someone across the hallway. We will go on mission trips overseas to rebuild houses, but we won't help clean-up the park in our own town. We will use our accounting skills to be the treasurer of an organization, but we won't help our brother-in-law with his taxes. We will call a friend from home to talk for hours, but we ignore the person down the hall who has no one to hang out with on Friday night. Even when we seek to love our neighbor, we are often just finding a way to love ourselves.

Self-centeredness is one of the deep flaws in human character; it is an indelible mark of our sinful state. We desperately want others to find us funny enough, or smart enough, or beautiful enough, or spiritual enough to be worthy of their love. I can't affirm you because I am so busy finding ways for you to affirm me. I can't serve you because I am longing for you to serve me. I can't love you because I so urgently need you to love me. How do we break this cycle of self-seeking desire? We return again to God, and we ground our being in his identity. We recognize first and foremost that we are beloved sons and daughters of the living God, that our identity is first in God, not in our relationship with other people. It is only when we recognize and accept that God loves us that we can be free to love others. But how do we work out this loving of neighbor in a practical way? What can I do to love my neighbor? Let me return now to the foot-rubbing and the coffee-bringing examples from the beginning and suggest that ordinary acts of kindness may be the most important way to work out the Great Commandment. The small, everyday choices that we make to put others' interests ahead of our own, to satisfy their needs before meeting our requirements, to think of them before thinking of the self. What might happen to a community in which kindness permeates the relationships?

Consider what happened to the British prisoners in the community of the prison camp in Chungkai, Thailand. Now, all of the new students know a bit about what happened in that prison camp because they were asked to read the book *To End All Wars* as part of orientation this fall. For the rest of you, let me briefly sketch the central action of the book to give you some context. The author, Ernest (or Ernie) Gordon is a Scottish soldier fighting against the Japanese during World War II. He is captured by the Japanese after the fall of Singapore and taken to a prison camp deep in the jungle of Thailand. The British prisoners are brought there to build a railroad through the jungle so that the Japanese will have a supply route to attack India. The Japanese were not signatories to the Geneva Convention, so they felt free to routinely torture, beat, starve, and work the British soldiers quite literally to death. Indeed, Japanese military culture viewed prisoners as subhuman because they had suffered the humiliation of surrender rather than committing suicide. As you might imagine, the camps are places of chaos and horror, and the prisoners initially live by the law of the survival of the fittest. As Ernie says in the book, "The weak were trampled underfoot, the sick ignored or resented, the dead forgotten,"[2] and he willingly participates in this world.

However, Ernie himself becomes sick with malaria, dysentery, and then diphtheria, eventually losing the use of his legs. He can't work, so he is taken to the hospital—what the prisoners call the death house—and he gives up all hope of living, even writing a final letter to his parents. Then two acquaintances, Dusty and Dinty, offer to build him a small hut outside of the hospital and agree to try to nurse him back to health. They feed him, wash him, give him words of comfort and encouragement, and he slowly recovers. Dusty is a Methodist, and Dinty is a Roman Catholic. They take care of Ernie at great cost to themselves, for they share their food with him and take care of him on top of all their other work.

Ernie is overwhelmed by the simple acts of human kindness, and there is a ripple effect that runs throughout the camp as the prisoners begin to look out for one another in very practical ways: the stronger share food with the weaker, the healthy make artificial limbs for the lame, the trained create medicines from plants for the sick. They love their neighbor in these very practical, redemptive ways, but they also love each in creative and intellectual ways. Ernie begins to teach classes and to organize a jungle university. They have courses in art, philosophy, literature, music, and theater—the liberal arts. They express love for one another by exercising the gifts of the mind.

The prisoners continue to suffer. They are still worked as slaves and their comrades still die in bunches, but the community offers hope through these selfless expressions of kindness and love. The prisoners' Christian ethic receives its ultimate test at the end of the memoir when the prisoners are confronted with wounded Japanese soldiers. It is one thing to love one's neighbors when they are your fellow prisoners who are suffering alongside you; it is quite another to love one's enemies, particularly when they have beaten, tortured, and starved you.

Now I hope that this brief description of the book will encourage you to read it in its entirety or perhaps watch the film version. I think the book is better than the film, but remember I teach English literature, so I always think the book is better than the film.

Ernie survives the war and returns to Scotland, but he has a difficult time settling back into "normal" life. In post-war Britain, he found that "everyone spoke of seeking security. But what did security mean but animal comfort, anaesthetized souls, closed minds and cold hearts? . . . In short, it meant a flight from God and descent into the hell of loneliness and despair."[3] Through all of the sacrifice, pain, and suffering of the prison camp, Ernie had found God, what he calls the "Infinitely Great." He had found a way to serve his neighbor, and he had found that by serving his neighbor he served his God and so lived a fulfilled life. He wanted to continue to live that fulfilled life in peace time, but he did not know in what context he could follow his intense longing to love God and neighbor as he did in the prison camp. He eventually finds what he is looking for in a university, and he serves as the dean of the chapel at Princeton University for twenty-five years.

Now I typically do not think of the university as a prison camp, but imagine with me what it might look like if the people of JBU would renew our collective commitment to love God and serve neighbor, what sort of ordinary acts of kindness would characterize this community. Could we be a place in which no one eats alone in the cafeteria because everyone has been invited to eat with others? Would we be a place in which roommates would volunteer to clean the bathroom to serve those in their suite? Could we be a place that changes the test scores in the Siloam Springs public schools because of the tutoring and love provided by JBU students? Could we be a place that cares more for people with AIDS in Arkansas and Africa than about who is sleeping with whom on the latest reality television show? We can and should be a people who are known by our acts of kindness and mercy to our neighbors.

But remember these acts of kindness are not limited to physical expressions of mercy. Could we be a place in which students encourage each other to enjoy class, even homework, rather than trying to get by with the least amount of academic work? Could we be a place in which the whole community celebrates the beauty found on the volleyball court, or in the concert performance, or at the art gallery? Could we be a place in which people care so much about truth and its close cousin doubt that our discussions about them would spill over from the classroom to the dorm room, from the student center to the homeless shelter, from the Bible study to the laboratory? We can and should be a place that is characterized by loving God with all of our heart, all of our soul, all of our mind, and all of our strength, and loving our neighbor as ourselves.

All of which brings me back to my foot-rubbing and coffee-bringing introduction. You see, there were two important jobs in the prison camp in order to take care of the sick: one was the job of the "masseuse teams" who would rub the feet and legs of sick patients in order to bring back their circulation and enable them to walk, and the second was the job of the food crew which brought the sick food and drink. In other words, it was foot-rubbing and coffee-bringing in the prison camp which brought hope, comfort, and love to the prisoners. These tasks literally brought life. Of course, this foot-rubbing and coffee-bringing should not be new to us. The same Christ who gave us the Great Commandment is the same Christ who—on the night that he was betrayed to the prison guards, on the night before he was tortured and killed, on the night before he healed our sin-sick souls—washed his disciples' feet and offered them wine and bread. These were the first-century acts of foot-rubbing and coffee-bringing that have brought us so much hope, comfort, and encouragement ever since. Indeed, they have brought us life.

May we too find ways to love God by rubbing feet and bringing coffee so that we and others may have life and have it abundantly.

May it always be true of us.

"Meeting in the Hall": Unity in the Church

Text: John 17:20-26

My prayer is not for them alone. I pray also for those who will believe in me through their message, that all of them may be one, Father, just as you are in me and I am in you. May they also be in us so that the world may believe that you have sent me. I have given them the glory that you gave me, that they may be one, as we are one. I in them and you in me. May they be brought to complete unity to let the world know that you sent me and have loved them even as you have loved me.

Father, I want those you have given me to be with me where I am, and to see my glory, the glory you have given me because you loved me before the creation of the world.

Righteous Father, though the world does not know you, I know you, and they know that you have sent me. I have made you known to them, and will continue to make you known in order that the love you have for me may be in them and that I myself may be in them.

In the preface to *Mere Christianity*, C. S. Lewis describes the project of his book by using the metaphor of a house. He says that "mere" Christianity is "like a hall out of which doors open into several rooms. If I can bring anyone into the hall I shall have done what I attempted. But it is in the rooms, not in the hall, that there are fires and chairs and meals. The hall is a place to wait in, a place from which to try the various doors, not a place to live in."[4] Lewis's metaphor is an apt one, I think, for this service and for the interdenominational character of JBU. We have come out of our rooms and are gathered in the hall to think and give witness to that which we affirm together as Christians, to affirm "mere Christianity." We rightfully spend most of our time living and working and worshiping in our rooms off that hallway. Those rooms are certainly different: some have large bathtubs while others have smaller sinks to wash us free from sin; some rooms are lined with bookcases while others have the latest software and computer technology; some rooms speak primarily in English, others in Spanish, and others in the languages of men and of angels. Some rooms keep careful track of their calendars and change their décor to match changes in the church seasons; others organize their rooms to maximize their flexibility of use by the church or the community; some rooms emphasis God's choice of us and others of our choice of God; some rooms leave their doors wide open to the hallway and others are more careful about entering and exiting their rooms.

These differences are real and important and not to be treated lightly, yet I would still contend that there is something, or more accurately Someone, who drew us into the hallway in the first place. Someone whom we can worship, and to whom we can collective give witness on days such as today. What we hold in common as Christians is not some vague, ambiguous belief, some lowest common denominator; it is, instead, the worship of, and witness to, the triune God who has been revealed most completely in the birth, life, death, and resurrection of Jesus Christ. And what we know of that God we know through the witness of Scripture and the teaching of the Holy Spirit. So, I would like to take a few moments to look at a passage in which Christ talks about our unity, about us gathering in the hall.

We should understand the context for the verses in John. Christ is in the upper room, and Judas has just left. Christ is talking with his disciples about his impending departure and death, and he finishes his teaching with this prayer of consecration in John 17. It is the longest and most detailed prayer of Christ recorded in Scripture. It is a prayer in which he gives over to his Father the responsibility and care for himself, for his immediate disciples, and for his future followers—for us. The situation would be similar to a soldier heading out to assignment in Iraq or perhaps a relief worker being pre-positioned in the path of a hurricane. You gather your family and friends together for final words of advice and encouragement, and you end the evening in prayer. John 17 is Christ's final extended prayer before his death. It is the end of that prayer, the section in which he prays for us, for "those who will believe in me," that I want to focus on today.

Unity: "All of them may be one."

The first thing that he prays for us is that "all of them may be one, Father, just as you are in me and I am in you." And later he repeats that desire asking for us to be "brought to complete unity." Ah, but here is the rub for us at JBU or in our city of Siloam Springs, which is reported to be in the *Guinness Book of World Records* for having more churches per capita than anywhere else in the United States. That Guinness record may just be an urban legend, but even if we do not own the record, a quick look in the phone book does suggest that we have our fair share of different churches, at least forty in my quick count. So how do we reconcile Christ's prayer for unity with our experience of the fragmentation in the church? Part of our response really should be confession for falling short of an ideal. We have all probably been involved in too many church splits or have spent too much time "shopping" from church to church. We are all broken and bent people, and we bring that brokenness into our church life. That brokenness causes disunity, and we should confess our failure. However, Christ also suggests the possibility of healthy diversity in his prayer for unity. He prays for a unity among believers that is similar to the unity of the Trinity. He prays that "all of them may be one, Father, *just as you are in me and I am in you.*" Now I am starting to tread near one of the great mysteries of our faith, the Trinity, that God is one God in three persons, a diversity of persons but unity of being. Our language breaks down as we seek to explain this mystery, but it does suggest that unity can involve some sense of difference, that perhaps we can be one church even as we worship on Saturday night or Sunday morning in different churches, that we worship the same Christ even if we worship in distinct ways. Again, this unity should not be characterized by a mindless blurring of all theological difference, but by the charitable, humble, obedient, and passionate following of Christ. We may not be one in every detail of what we believe, but perhaps we can be one in whom we follow and serve. It is the mystery of the unity of the church, a mystery reflected, partially and imperfectly, in unity services and interdenominational universities, but also whenever two or three are gathered in his name and he is there in their midst.

Witness: "So that the world may believe"

John goes on to suggest that the unity of believers is a witness to the world of the reality of Christ's message, a witness to the reality that Christ has been sent by God. Christ prays, "may they also be in us so that the world may believe that you have sent me," and then, later, "may they be brought to complete unity to let the world know that you sent me." In other words, our unity as followers of Christ bears witness in the world to his authority as the son of God. When we slander, or ridicule, or dismiss, or disparage others in the family of faith, we make it harder for those outside the faith to believe that Christ was sent by God. When we partner with, or praise, or encourage others in the faith, we testify to the world that Christ is real in our lives and in this world, that he is the son of God whom we follow.

Love: "You have loved them even as you have loved me."

Moreover, Christ also tells us in this prayer that our unity reflects the love that God has for us and for him. In verse 23 he prays, "May they be brought to complete unity to let the world know" that God sent his son, Jesus Christ, but also to let the world know that God loved us even as he loved his son. Then again, in verse 26, Christ says, "I have made you known to them and will continue to make you known in order that the love you have for me may be in them." It is a staggering fact. The God of the universe has chosen to love us as his sons and daughters; he loves us as much as he loves his own son. Our unity in the faith is a unity of being in the same family and being loved by the same Father. We can stand together knowing that all who follow Christ are beloved children of the living God. And, while no two children in a family are exactly alike in their appearance, skills, inclinations, faults, or desires, each shares the unity of belonging to the same family.

Of course, God's love for us is neither cheap nor sentimental. God expresses his love for us at great cost, at the cost of the death of his son. So if Christ asks for God to love us even as he loved him, we should recognize that God's love can be demanding, can ask for sacrifice, can ask us to spend our lives for the benefit of others. And, our unity in Christ is often expressed in that sacrifice of love for others. As Christ commands in Luke, we should love the Lord our God with all our heart and with all of our soul and with all of our strength and with all of our mind, and we should love our neighbors as ourselves.

For instance, while a famous former Arkansas politician said that it takes a village to raise a child, it really takes unity in the church to raise our children, and there is evidence of that unity in this town. I don't know about your children, but occasionally my kids do not always want to listen to Carey and me, particularly after their thirteenth birthdays. Indeed, my kids now have a common response when I start to offer words of advice; they roll their eyes, offer a world-weary sigh, and say, "Dad, is this another one of your life lessons?" However, I also know that my own children have been mentored, loved, and challenged by youth groups or Bible studies led by people from four different churches and by undergraduates from JBU. Carey and I are deeply grateful for the way others have stepped into the lives of our children and borne witness to the reality of Christ in their lives. Moreover, it is what we try to do at JBU as we partner with families and educate young people to take on the faith as their own in their careers, their families, and their communities. I also know that many of you in the churches help us in this work, particularly with our international students who are far from home: you invite them to your homes for meals; you take them into your family life; and you offer to store their stuff during the summer time. As Christ says in Mark, "Let the little children come to me, and do not hinder them, for the kingdom of God belongs to such as these" (10:14). As one church, we should keep on keeping on and expand our service to young people.

I also think that we reflect our unity in Christ in our service to those in need in our community. St. Francis Clinic provides health care and advocacy support to the uninsured in our community. Genesis House provides transitional financial help and other support resources such as transportation, Internet access, showers, and meals to help keep individuals and families in their homes or to help them get into a home. The Manna Center collects and distributes food and clothing and offers referral services for people in need. New Beginnings Pregnancy Center offers education, emotional and spiritual support, lay counseling, and other resources to help women facing difficulties because of a pregnancy. And there are a host of other organizations like these in Siloam Springs. Each of them depends on volunteer support from people who come from so many of the different churches. Moreover, many of the people who need help from these organizations do not feel comfortable entering our churches because of their struggles to survive. The first place that they will witness the truth of Christ is in these organizations that are meeting their basic needs, and one of the things that they will see in entering those places is the unity of the church. As Christ says in Matthew 25:40, "Whatever you did for one of the least of these brothers of mine, you did for me." As one church, we should keep on keeping on and expand our service to those in need.

So, we are one church in caring for people and in caring for those in need, but perhaps we can also be one church in other ways. For instance, I think that we are one church at times in giving glory to God through the arts. The First United Methodist Church generously provides space to the Sager Arts Center. The Chorale of Ozarks brings together voices from all different church choirs to sing praise to our one God. And JBU's Cathedral Choir opens the Advent season for the whole community with its glorious Candlelight Christmas service. I can also imagine other ways that we could be seen as exhibiting unity in our following of Christ. Perhaps we could be one church in our taking care of God's beautiful creation in town, or in the way we are hospitable to strangers who come to Siloam, or in helping people recover from their addictions, or in creating new businesses that provide jobs for the unemployed. God makes his claim on our whole world, so we should not be shy about looking for new places to follow him as one church.

So, in Lewis's terms, we have come together to meet in the hall. And, while I agree with him that we live, worship, and work primarily in our different rooms in the house, it is good for us to meet every once in awhile in the hall. It bears witness to the God we love and who loves us. But we should also not wait to meet in the hall once every few years and only in big groups. We should meet each other in smaller groups and find common work in the hall all the time by serving the teenagers in youth groups, or people in need at the homeless shelter, or in a musical performance at Sager Arts Center. As we sing and worship today, as we sort clothes or counsel a patient tomorrow, as we encourage a lonely pregnant woman or make a contribution to a health clinic next week, we should remember that there is a whole world watching our work in the hall through the windows. As Lewis says, even if we do not live in the hall, if we bring new people into the hall, then they will have an easier time finding their way to the doors of the individual rooms.

And, finally and most importantly, we should never forget that the main door into the house remains red because we only come into the house of God through the blood Christ shed on the cross. So, let us heed the prayer of Christ that we be brought to complete unity so that we might bear witness to others that "God so loved the world that he gave his one and only son, that whoever believes in him shall not perish but have eternal life."

May that always be true of us as one church.

CHAPTER 2

First Semester

Who Am I? Beloved Child of God

Part of the accepted narrative of the university years is that they are the time and place when young people "discover" themselves, when they form their identities separate from their parents, when they come to "try on" beliefs, values, professions, relationships, and commitments to see if they "fit" their growing sense of self. Indeed, I often find it fascinating to talk with students about their conscious efforts to "reinvent" themselves on coming to college. They request a roommate from a different country to learn about the world. They refuse to wear any item of clothing that identifies their high school. They completely change the color of their hair or get tattoos. They volunteer for clubs, or organizations, or activities that they have never tried before. They go to churches far different from ones that they grew up in. Some of them move far from home to experience a different part of the country. In some cases, they even change their names, often adopting their middle names instead of their first names, to mark a break with their past. While young people certainly do begin to understand and articulate better who they are during their university years, I think that the traditional narrative of university life exaggerates the amount of freedom that we have as individuals to "remake" ourselves. A thoroughly biblical sense of anthropology suggests that human beings are fundamentally shaped by being made in the image of God so that the question of our identity can only be fully answered in our relationship to God. Moreover, our families have a large influence on whom we can become. Chapel allows me to explore with students how Scripture answers those deeper questions of identity, and I often find that it is important to address that topic during the fall semester.

The section begins with a chapel reflection in which I describe my own conversion experience and church upbringing as a model for how our pasts shape who we are in Christ. Even though the "testimonial" has an honored place in our Christian traditions, I was still surprised how students responded to this talk. Many of them, too, felt uneasy about their "boring" testimonies and appreciated my affirmation of the blessings of growing up in a faithful family and church. The second sermon in this section was intentionally paired with the first. While the church is often willing to hear our testimonies of faith, we don't seem as ready to listen to stories of doubt. I expect that is because we are afraid that stories of doubt will spread more doubt in the mind of the audience. However, I have found that it is essential to allow space for stories of doubt, particularly when working with university students. As they grapple with the problem of evil, effects of poverty, other world religions, or with personal trauma and loss, they need to hear how others have struggled to understand God in those life experiences. They need to hear that it is okay for Christians to echo the Father in Mark 9:24, "Lord, I do believe. Help me overcome my unbelief." The stories of faith and of doubt are essential to understanding who we are as followers of Jesus Christ.

Sexuality is also clearly one of the more important topics that students want to discuss as they come to grapple with their sense of identity. Presenting a biblical understanding of sexuality in the highly sexualized world of contemporary culture is a challenge. The third sermon in this section seeks to respond to that challenge.

Sexuality is only one area in which we can fail to understand ourselves correctly. In the fourth reflection, I consider how important it is generally to understand ourselves as sinners, as 500 denarii sinners, to have a clear view of our own identity and our need for confession and dependence on God. In the final reflection, I think through what it means to know that God calls us by name. As followers of Jesus Christ, we begin to answer the question of "who am I" by recognizing that we are first the beloved children of the living God, a recognition as relevant to the nineteen-year-old getting a new piercing as to the seventy-nine-year-old in the retirement home.

"Come and Listen"

Text: Psalm 66:16-20

Come and listen, all you who fear God, let me tell you what he has done for me. I cried out to him with my mouth; his praise was on my tongue. If I had cherished sin in my heart, the Lord would not have listened; but God has surely listened and heard my voice in prayer. Praise be to God, who has not rejected my prayer or withheld his love from me!

The theme for chapel this semester is "Telling the Stories of Faith," and I am looking forward to hearing the stories of our speakers this semester. If you are like me, you have grown up in the church or have been to summer camp or been involved in youth ministries, and you are familiar with the genre of the faith story or the testimony. Often, particularly in the camp setting, the sharing of testimonies occurs late at night around a campfire. As you sat in the dark, you would often hear dramatic stories of conversion, the best of which often had a certain narrative shape to them. First, the person would describe, sometimes in great gory detail, the ugliness of their own sin or the effects of sin in their lives. They would be deeply involved in stealing, or gangs, or drugs, or pornography, or would have suffered from cancer or a car accident. Then, often with the help of a youth minister or pastor or camp counselor, they come to recognize the depth of their own sin, the consequences of that sin being hell, and Christ's offer of love and forgiveness. They would then describe a turning away from sin toward Christ, a dramatic conversion to a new life that is almost exactly opposite to their early life. These stories are often inspiring both in their details and the transformation in people's lives. And, of course, these stories have biblical precedent—the conversion of Saul to Paul, from the person who persecutes the Christians to the person blinded on the road to Damascus, from the person holding the coats for those killing Stephen to the follower of Christ writing much of the New Testament.

Now, again, if you were at all like me, you would sit in the dark and say to yourself—darn, my story of conversion is so boring. Perhaps you, like me, suffer from what I call "Boring Testimony Syndrome." Sure, I know that I am a sinner, but my sins are common and boring—not pornography but pride, not stealing but indifference to the poor, not gangs but gossip, not drugs but selfishness. Moreover, while I am committed to Christ, I don't always see dramatic evidence of that commitment—no blinding lights on the road, no detox programs, no conversion of my gang friends, no writing of letters to the churches in Philippi. Instead, the narrative arc of my life has been much more ordinary. God has filled my life with good things: a loving family, educational opportunities, good churches, meaningful work, health, food, recreation. Yet, I am still often mired in petty sins and my times of doubt are often more intense and more frequent than my times of faith. Indeed, sometimes the blessings intensify the doubts because I feel as if I need to earn those blessings in order to enjoy them, and I know that I haven't earned them. In fact, the doubts seem to be evidence that I have not mustered enough faith to deserve the blessings. It can be a vicious cycle.

Our theme verse for the semester comes from Psalm 66:16: "Come and listen, all you who fear God; let me tell you what he has done for me." The psalmist recognizes that God works both through times of faith and times of doubt to bring us to himself. The psalm is split into two parts: the first twelve verses are a collective hymn sung by the people of Israel, and the last eight verses are an individual hymn of the psalmist. In the collective hymn, the people of Israel sing of how God remained faithful to them through times of rescue and times of testing. In verses 5-6, the psalmist reminds them of the Exile, the rescue from Egypt, and slavery: "Come and see what God has done, how awesome his works in man's behalf! He turned the sea into dry land, they passed through the waters on foot—come let us rejoice in him." However, in verses 10-12, he also reminds them of times of testing: "For you, O God, tested us, you refined us like silver. You brought us into prison and laid burdens on our backs. You let men ride over our heads; we went through fire and water, but you brought us to a place of abundance." The psalmist recognizes that God also uses trials to bring about his purposes among the people of Israel. And what is true at the collective level is also true at the individual level. The psalmist comes to God's temple with "vows my lips promised and my mouth spoke when I was in trouble," but he is also convinced that "God has surely listened and heard my voice in prayer" (66:14, 19). So, when we come to testify, when we come to tell what God has done for us, we should be ready to give witness and praise both for the moments of rescue and blessing, and for the moments of testing and doubt. I know that God has used both moments of faith and times of doubt to bring me closer to him. Today, I would like to tell you a few of the stories about those moments of faith in my life, particularly from my childhood. Later in the semester, I will share with you my stories of doubt.

Blessings of Family

One of those blessings of faith for me was being born into a family of believers. As far back as I know, my family has been committed Christians, a blessing for which I have increasingly become grateful as I have grown older. Moreover, my own initial commitment to Christ was largely shaped by my family. It happened on August 7 1970, when I was seven years old. Yes, I am one of those people who have a date that I can write in my Bible as my spiritual "birthday." However, I have a deep respect for those who speak of their faith as a growing awareness of their commitment to Christ and who cannot point to any one moment of conversion. God works in our lives in a variety of ways, so we should expect that our stories of faith would have a great variety.

We were on a family vacation in the northern woods of Wisconsin. We were staying with my grandparents in a cabin next to a lake. The cabin came with use of a boat, and my father, ten-year-old sister, and I decided to take the boat to a nearby island for an overnight camping trip. As you might expect, I could hardly wait for this exciting adventure to begin. However, when we went down to the boat in the late afternoon, we discovered the tilt on the motor was not working, so we would not be able to land the boat on the beach of the island without ruining the motor. I was desperately disappointed, so my Dad decided to try to salvage the evening by setting up a campsite right there next to the boat dock. It sounded pretty lame to me, but what alternative did I have? So we set up the tent and collected wood for the campfire.

As we were roasting our hot dogs and eating chips, my sister began to talk about her experience at Bible camp. In particular, she talked about a friend who had been "saved" during her time at camp. Feeling a bit left out of the conversation, I blurted out that I was saved too. My sister in all of her fifth-grade sophistication and superiority looked at me quite skeptically, quickly corrected my theological error, and then explained in a matter-of-fact way its significance: "I don't think that you are saved, which means, of course, that you are going to hell and it will be as hot as that campfire." As you might imagine, I was a bit shaken by my sister's revelation, and I thought that this day was definitely going downhill. I had woken that morning with plans for an exciting overnight on an island, and now my sister had just informed me that I was going to spend the rest of eternity separated from God in hellish flames.

My Dad wisely intervened and explained the gospel simply by quoting from John and Romans. With those scriptural passages, he explained about our sinfulness and need of salvation, of Christ's death and resurrection as an act of love and as the means to bring about that salvation, and our response as one of faith in Christ's work and obedience to his authority. Then we prayed together for Christ to become both Savior and Lord in my life. I was so excited about the decision that I ran back to the cabin and told my mother and grandparents. We ended up abandoning the camping trip and slept back in the cabin that night. There was no dramatic change in my life. I returned home to second grade, rec-league basketball, and church on Sunday. I am still grateful, however, to point to that conversation as the beginning of my following of Jesus Christ. Moreover, while I am still not so sure about my sister's motives in declaring my eternal destiny, I am deeply grateful to God to be born into a family of faith that was ready to give witness to my need for Christ.

Blessings of Learning

The next spiritual blessing that I remember was a book recommendation. I know that too sounds incredibly nerdy, or at least boring, but I love to read and God has taught me so much about himself and his world through the books that I have read. I remember when I was ten years old and Margaret Schneider introduced me to *The Hobbit* in the basement library of Longfellow school. I read it in a week, and the rest of the Tolkien's trilogy in a month. I was both deeply saddened and deeply satisfied when I came to the end. I was saddened that there was not more to read about this adventure and satisfied because it was a story that rang of truth: the truth of courage against overwhelming odds, the truth of friendship being more important than accomplishment, the truth of self-sacrifice bringing about redemption. Moreover, it was a story with great battles, magic rings, elusive elves, fierce orcs, walking trees, and, most importantly, a story with the ultimate victory of good over evil by means that no one would expect. Frodo follows his calling, supported by his friend Sam, extending mercy to Gollum, and defeating overwhelming evil. Even though I didn't realize it at the time, Tolkien's story echoed the gospel story that was becoming central in my own life. God has used books ever since to teach me about himself and his world.

God also used teachers to help me understand himself and his world. I remember my high school English teacher who would sit cross-legged on his desk and laugh with delight at the puns in Shakespeare. Or the Greek teacher in college who would deepen our understanding of a verse by explaining the significance of a verb tense. Or the English professor whose lectures on Homer were as insightful about what it means to be human as any sermon that I had ever heard. Or the philosophy professor who made belief in Christ a reasonable, and not simplistic, proposition in the history of ideas. These teachers had a passion to understand Christ in all things and were not satisfied with easy answers from themselves or from their students. Their passion for learning and for faith was infectious, and that passion clearly shaped the direction of my own life. I am deeply grateful to God for the teachers that he has brought into my life. They have been one of life's great blessings.

Blessings of Church

Church was also a central part of my growing up. I know, boring again. We went almost every Sunday from nine to twelve. The first hour was a communion service, the second hour was Sunday school, and the third hour was preaching. Those mornings felt long, very long, when I was a young boy, and I can't say that I remembered a lot of specific content from the sermons or the Sunday school classes afterward. However, I do remember many of the memory verses that I learned during Sunday school. I do remember one of the elders in the church who would regularly get choked up with tears as he shared what God had been teaching him. And I do remember the smell of the potluck suppers as we would gather around the folding tables in the church basement. I do remember the cold water in the baptismal pool when I was baptized at twelve. And I remember sitting with my grandmother in church and having her give me a hard candy to pass the time. I also remember her funeral service in that same church. But what I most remember is being asked to serve in the church—to be a shepherd in the Christmas pageant, to give devotions in youth group, to teach a Sunday school class, to run the boys' floor-hockey club, even to preach a sermon as a young college student. Church was a place to serve, not just a place to go. That challenge to serve was a great encouragement to my spiritual life even if I didn't always recognize or appreciate it at the time, and I am grateful to God for the blessing of that challenge.

The other lasting church memory for me was the weekly communion service. It was an unscripted service. It would start with an opening prayer, and then someone might suggest the singing of a hymn, and another person would read a Scripture and explain it, and then perhaps volunteer another hymn or prayer, and so on. There were often periods of silence, sometimes for as long as five to ten minutes. The service would always conclude with the passing of the bread and the wine. As a young boy, I was often bored and distracted during the service. However, as I grew older, I came to appreciate its rhythms better. I came to see how the hymns and scriptural reflections would often build on one another, how the silence would often serve as an important counterpoint to the speaking—a time for Christ to speak to us instead of us speaking about him. I also became increasingly aware of how the momentum of the service culminated in the taking of the bread and drinking from the cup. All of our talk ended in this simple action; all of the singing ended in this collective movement; all of the mess of our individual lives united and reconciled in this tangible act of participating together in Christ's life, death, and resurrection.

So, as the theme verse suggests, come and listen, all you who fear God, and let me tell you what he has done for me. Come and listen, even to my boring testimony about family, books, teachers, and church, because God has shown his faithfulness to me and, I expect, to many of you, in those ordinary things. Come and listen to the stories of faith from others in whom God has been at work. You may respond to those stories with sympathy because they resonate with your own life, with skepticism because they do not, with longing for God to do more in your life, or with fear because he may be doing too much. Perhaps you will respond by telling your own story, even if it is boring, to your friends, or your family, or even a stranger.

Most of your responses to the stories this semester will be private, between you and God, which is okay. However, as I learned in all of those Sunday morning communion services growing up, Christ does not only call us to come and listen; he also calls us to take and eat, to give testimony to our hope in the risen Christ by eating the bread and drinking the cup. In communion we give witness to our decision to follow Christ, a calling that I first heard clearly some forty years ago on the edge of a lake in northern Wisconsin, and a calling that has made all the difference in my ordinary and flawed life. So, JBU, on this cold morning at the beginning of a new semester, let us not just come and listen; let us also take and eat and commit ourselves again to live out our witness to Jesus Christ, our Lord and Savior, in thought, word, affection, and deed. "For whenever you eat this bread and drink this cup, you proclaim the Lord's death until he comes" (1 Cor. 11:26).

May it always be true of us.

Doubt

Text: John 20:19-31

On the evening of that first day of the week, when the disciples were together, with the doors locked for fear of the Jews, Jesus came and stood among them and said, "Peace be with you!" After he said this, he showed them his hands and side. The disciples were overjoyed when they saw the Lord.

Again, Jesus said. "Peace be with you! As the father has sent me, I am sending you." And with that he breathed on them and said, "Receive the Holy Spirit. If you forgive anyone his sins, they are forgiven; if you do not forgive them, they are not forgiven."

Now Thomas (called Didymus), one of the Twelve, was not with the disciples when Jesus came. So the other disciples told him "We have seen the Lord!"

But he said to them, "Unless I see the nail marks in his hands and put my finger where the nails were, and put my hand into his side, I will not believe it."

A week later his disciples were in the house again, and Thomas was with them. Though the doors were locked, Jesus came and stood among them and said, "Peace be with you!" Then he said to Thomas, "Put your finger here, see my hands. Reach out your hand and put it into my side. Stop doubting and believe."

Thomas said to him, "My Lord and my God!"

Then Jesus told him, "Because you have seen me, you have believed; blessed are those who have not seen and yet have believed."

Now students may remember that I started the chapel series this semester by telling my "testimony," my story of coming to faith in Jesus

Christ in the northern woods of Wisconsin, and then having God teach me through family, books, teachers, and church. Today, I would like to tell you about the times of doubt in my life and how this story of Thomas has helped me to think about doubt and its role in faith.

First, however, I want to illustrate two different ways to conceive of faith. You could consider this part of my talk as equivalent to the "children's sermon," which is often my favorite part of the Sunday morning service. And, like any good children's sermon, I need to get out my visual aid—these wooden building blocks.

One way to conceive of faith is as more of a linear process. You understand certain key principles about God, about Christ's death and resurrection, about the authority of Scripture, and you build on those key principles as you come to other understandings about baptism, or speaking in tongues, or the importance of taking care of the poor, or being concerned for creation. You slowly build up your tower of faith—sort of like what I have done here with my tower of wood blocks. Now there is a difficulty with the approach because new experiences come into your life: you read Scripture from a different perspective after you have been on a mission trip; you hear something different in Old Testament class; or you come to grips with grief in your family. All of sudden you want to move one of your blocks in your tower. Pretend that this block represents your view of the Christian's response to those in need. You grew up in a church where it wasn't spoken of much, but then you go on JBU's mission trip to Ethiopia and you are confronted with desperate poverty, and you think that you need to move this block closer to the base foundation of your tower of faith. So you try to move it, and all of the blocks collapse; you have a crisis of faith. You rebuild your tower of blocks, but then you meet your roommate who was sprinkled as a baby yet seems to be a deeply committed Christian. You have grown up believing in believer's baptism, and you still do, but it is not as close to the base foundation truths of the faith, so you want to move this block higher on the tower. So again you try to move this block and the stack falls. Clearly you can rebuild and rebuild the stack, but it is a pretty brittle structure and almost seems set up for regular collapses.

I think that there is an alternative way to conceive of how we put together our principles of faith, one that is more spatial than linear, one that is more resilient than brittle, one that may be more faithful to living in a world made good by God but broken by our sin. Instead of building a tower of faith with the core blocks in the foundation and building vertically, you arrange the core blocks in the center of a constellation of blocks and move out horizontally. The core principles have to be in the center: the birth, death, and physical resurrection of Christ; the authority of Scripture; the importance of the church; and the Trinity and the Incarnation. But the secondary principles, important but debatable, are further from that center circle. Now in this model, when a new principle or experience comes into your life, such as your mission trip to the developing world, you can include a new block that may influence the positions of all of the other blocks but the whole structure doesn't entirely collapse. In this model, you may even shift a block to a new position (say start going to a Pentecostal church instead of a Baptist church) and test out how the blocks move without having to go through an entire collapse. Moreover, if I am remembering my science right, all of the blocks have a force of attraction to one another, so they move in unity and coherence. If you shift this block here, then these three will shift that way.

In the first model, every block has to remain in its exact place or you have a crisis of faith. In this second model, the central blocks are essential—they serve to center and ground your whole faith—but there is some expectation of shifting in the periphery. The shifting has an effect, and it can be painful, but the whole structure realigns after the shift into a new coherence with the center still being the center. There is not a complete rebuilding each time. I would suggest that this second model offers a more robust, healthy, and resilient way to conceive of the faith in a world created by God but broken by sin.

Let me tell you about one of my periods of doubt. I was at Oxford studying English literature and literary theory, and I would ride my bike every day some two miles to the Bodleian library to read for the better part of eight hours. The Bodleian library is old; the first part of it was constructed in 1488 and rededicated in 1602. The Bodleian also works in a unique way. There are very few open stacks from which you could get a book yourself. Instead, you would write a request on a piece of paper, and then they would bring you the book from stacks that were behind the walls or under the courtyard. It typically took four to five hours for them to find the book (Oxford is not known for its efficiency). In other sections of the library, the books are chained to the stacks, and have been for over four hundred to five hundred years, at first because the books were rare and therefore valuable, and now because the books are old and therefore valuable. Several of the library scenes in the Harry Potter movies are set in the older parts of the Bodleian library, which may help give you some sense of what I am describing.

It was the summer of 1989, and I was reading the works of Jacques Derrida in the Upper Reading room of the Bodleian. I had a regular spot in the library, next to one of the stained-glass windows. Without going through all of the boring details, I had been reading Derrida for about a week. He does not just make a rational argument for skepticism; instead, he enacts his skepticism in the way that he plays with language. In his early work, he questions our capacity to communicate or know with any certainty, suggesting that all we can do is play with language. His arguments are persuasive and spellbinding when seen from a certain perspective, and I was enthralled with the reading. Then, one afternoon, I thought of the ramification of the skepticism—if we cannot trust language to communicate, if we can't know anything beyond language, how can we know anything about God or other people, or about Christ's resurrection? Is my faith just the ever deferring and differing language of my own imagination? As I began to contemplate the full ramifications, I literally felt like I was going to throw up, which would have been awkward in any library but particularly in one that was five hundred years old and did not have a toilet nearby. My blocks had collapsed, and I doubted pretty much everything that I had grown up believing, not just about faith, but about life.

It took the better part of six months for me to work through this particular time of doubt, and it was a dark time for me although not many people realized it—not even Carey. I continued to live out my faith, but the big questions gnawed away in the corner of my mind as I sang in church or told a Bible story to my son. It was through the help of a friend, a friend who did not dismiss the reasonableness of the doubt, but who gave testimony to his faith with his doubt, who helped me the most. I don't have time to give the full explanation of how I wrestled with this question, but suffice it to say I was comforted by Anslem's claim that I don't understand in order to believe, but believe in order to understand—that we have a faith seeking understanding, that faith precedes knowledge for all people. And, I was convinced even more so by Kierkegaard's claim about our need to leap to faith, the leap being terrifying even to the point of nausea, but also exhilarating because the stakes were so high and the results were so important. Belief in Christ truly is an all or nothing proposition, and time and time again in my periods of doubt, God has given me faith to choose Christ. Times of doubt had made my faith more vital and all-encompassing.

I didn't solve the problem of doubt in this one experience; doubt persists in my life of faith even now, and I expect that it will to the end of my days. Through doubt, God sharpens my dependence on faith in him. I have found that John's account of Thomas has helped me in my periods of doubt, so let's turn again to that story and focus on some key phrases.

On that first day

Christ appears to the disciples on Easter Sunday evening, and it is the first day of a whole new creation. Christ has returned in his new resurrected body. It is quite a body: it still bears the marks of his life before death—the wounds in his hands and his side—but it is also a body that seemingly can pass through locked doors. This new body is clearly physical—Christ invites Thomas to touch him, and Christ will eat with the disciples—but it is physicality that is not restrained by our current limitations. It is the new body of the new creation, and it is serves as a signal to us of what we have to hope for in the resurrection of the dead.

Indeed, when Christ breathes on the disciples and they receive the Holy Spirit, his act echoes the first creation when God breathed on Adam and Eve in order to give them life. His resurrection gives testimony to the new life that we have been promised; it is the new creation for which we live in hope; it is a sign of the new body that we will receive in the last days. And, notice, Christ's example suggests that our new bodies will also carry the marks of life before death, that what happens in this world will be reflected in what happens in the next, that there will be a continuity of our identity into the new heaven and the new earth. How this works itself out is a mystery, I think, but a wonderful mystery that gives significance to our lives now, for what we do now will likely have eternal effects. Easter truly is the first day of a new world and a new hope for human beings.

Thomas was not with the disciples.

Some people gather together when they face difficult times; others seek to be alone with their grief and disappointment. Thomas is of the second sort. He wants to think through this loss by himself. He wants to be alone to come to grips with what has happened over the previous week. And what has happened is not what he expected. From every indication, Thomas and the other disciples held the standard Jewish expectations for the Messiah. The Messiah was supposed to restore the nation of Israel to its proper place in the world. A faithful Jew, even one who had spent the last three years with Jesus, would never have expected the Messiah to die and still be the Messiah. Thomas was bitterly disappointed, not just from the sorrow of losing his teacher, but because Christ did not live up to his expectations. Thomas had committed himself to this cause for three years of his life, living on the road, abandoning his work, and sacrificing to be a part of this movement, and it had failed. The Roman oppressors had won again.

We too have expectations of Christ that are not always in keeping with his truth. We pray, rightfully so, for healing or for a job or for a spouse or for direction, and sometimes what Christ offers is not what we expect. He responds with mercy instead of healing, with friendship instead of marriage, with dependence instead of employment, or even with silence as an answer. Like Thomas, we want a Messiah who will fix the brokenness of this world and fix it now. Restore the kingdom now. Overthrow the oppressors now. Heal the sick now. Comfort the lonely now. When Christ doesn't meet our expectations, we tend to doubt his trustworthiness rather than to look again at our expectations and their timing.

"Unless I see"

Thomas is not ready to hear the testimony of the other disciples about Christ's resurrection. If he did not expect the Messiah to die, he has even less expectation that the Messiah will be raised from the dead. He has already been disappointed once; he certainly is not going to be taken in again. So, he asks for verification; he wants physical evidence of this resurrection; he basically says to his friends and to Christ—prove it.

Whatever you may think of Thomas's brash declaration of doubt, at least he is focused on the right question. He wants to know if Jesus has risen physically from the dead, and that is clearly the most important question. If Christ has not risen from the dead, it doesn't really matter what the Bible teaches on creation, or alcohol, or sexuality, or the poor, or anything else. If he has risen from the dead, it makes all the difference in the world. So, if you are questioning the Christian faith, take your doubt seriously and question first the central proposition about the resurrection before you get enmeshed in the secondary issues. Figure out what you believe about the core claims about Jesus, before you reject Christianity for less important issues. Determine if you can place the central blocks into your circle before you start worrying about the blocks at the margins.

There are good intellectual and historical reasons to believe that the Gospels are reliable texts, that they give clear witness to Christ's resurrection, and that Christ's actual resurrection is the best explanation for the rise of the early church. I don't have time for the full argument, but if you wanted to explore this issue more, I would highly recommend Timothy Keller's *Reason for God: Belief in the Age of Skepticism*. Let me offer a couple of arguments from the book. For instance, most of the early eyewitnesses of Christ's resurrection were women. Women were held in such low social esteem in first-century Palestine that their testimony was not allowed in court. If the Gospels were made up, there would be no incentive to claim that women were the first to see Christ, other than the fact that they actually did see him. Or, take another example. Neither in the Greco-Roman world nor the Jewish world would the resurrection of Jesus make philosophical sense. In the Greco-Roman world, the spirit was good and the material body was corrupt. As Keller suggests, any resurrection of the material body "was not only impossible, but totally undesirable."[1] In the time of Jesus, some Jews had come to hope that in the future there would be a bodily resurrection of all the righteous when God renewed the entire world. However, they would have never thought of the resurrection of a single person in the midst of history while sickness and death continued. In other words, the physical resurrection of an individual in the midst of history to bring about the justice of God was not a readily available story line in the worldviews of the day. It is at least as reasonable to think that it actually happened as it is to think that the Gospel writers were particularly imaginative folks who came up with this new idea.

There are plenty more intellectual, philosophical, and historical grounds for believing in the reality of the resurrection, and I would encourage you to explore them in more depth. Examining the arguments for and against the resurrection has helped me see that the belief in the resurrection is a reasonable proposition—I don't have to turn off my mind to be Christian; but, that it is also not a necessary conclusion—I can understand how others may examine these arguments and may not be convinced. The honest skeptic does exist, and I respect his or her unbelief, in no small part because doubt has been so intertwined with faith in my own life. Belief in Christ is an imminently reasonable truth, but it is more than just reasonable; it is also an existential truth that makes sense of the suffering in this broken world, and that is why it is convincing to me.

"Put your finger here."

Let me explain by returning to Thomas. Christ is merciful to Thomas, and he answers Thomas's challenge to "prove it" by appearing again a week later. In graphic detail, Christ offers his wounds as physical evidence to answer Thomas's intellectual doubts: "Put your finger here, see my hands. Reach out your hand and put it into my side. Stop doubting and believe." Christ offers a reason for Thomas to believe. Some of you may be thinking, if only he would do the same for me, if only he would appear to me, or speak audibly to me, perhaps just give my dad a job, or heal my friend with cancer. If Christ would give me some visual or tactile or life evidence of his resurrection, then all of my intellectual doubts about Christianity would be put away. Christ anticipates our thoughts and responds by offering his final beatitude, his final blessing: "Because you have seen me, you have believed; blessed are those that have not seen and yet have believed." We are blessed because we believe even though we have not seen.

But why should we believe if we don't see? And here, I think, is the central, existential truth of the resurrection revealed in this gospel story. Christ certainly offers Thomas his wounds as physical evidence, as logical arguments, as intellectual reasons to believe in the resurrection, but he also offers his wounds as wounds, as his experience of the suffering and the pain of living in this world, as his witness that he understands existentially the grief, despair, doubt, and ache of living in this world broken by sin. Christ does not respond to our doubt only with logical arguments; he responds with the story of his life and that story includes suffering. It is a story in which he too knows what it feels like to be forsaken, abandoned, and bereft of his belief in God. "My God, My God, why have you forsaken me?"

If Christ responded to my doubt only with intellectual arguments, I am not sure that I could make the leap to faith because intellectual arguments do not always help me in tough moments of life: moments when my son asks about the justice of God in the instance of the three-year-old with a brain tumor in an orphanage in Guatemala City; when our chaplain tells me that he has skin cancer; when a colleague and friend speaks of the surgery for his young child; when another friend loses his wife or a student loses his father; or when a brother is betrayed by a spouse or a colleague loses the ability to teach. Intellectual arguments are important but they are not enough for me in those existential moments. Instead, I cling to the fact that Christ offers Thomas his wounds, the evidence of his suffering, because those wounds remind us that Christ knows and feels and understands and has compassion for our suffering, even the suffering of our doubt. That is a Messiah I can follow, a Messiah that I can turn to in times of doubt and in times of faith—a Messiah from whom we can hear the command to stop doubting and believe and to whom we can reply, with Thomas: "My Lord and my God."

For, as it says in Hebrews 4:14-16: "Therefore since we have a great high priest who has gone through the heavens, Jesus the Son of God, let us hold firmly to the faith we profess. For we do not have a high priest who is unable to sympathize with our weaknesses, but we have one who has been tempted in every way, just as we are—yet was without sin. Let us then approach the throne of grace with confidence so that we may receive mercy and find grace to help us in our time of need."

May it always be true of us.

Flesh of My Flesh

Text: Genesis 1:27; 2:18-25

So God created man in his own image, in the image of God he created him; male and female he created them. . . .

The Lord God said, "It is not good for the man to be alone. I will make a helper suitable for him."

Now the Lord God had formed out of the ground all the beasts of the field and all the birds of the air. He brought them to the man to see what he would name them; and whatever the man called each living creature, that was his name. So the man gave names to all the livestock, the birds of the air and all of the beasts of the field.

But for Adam no suitable helper was found. So the Lord God caused the man to fall into a deep sleep; and while he was sleeping, he took one of the man's ribs and closed up the place with flesh. Then the Lord God made a woman from the rib he had taken out of the man, and he brought her to the man.

The man said,
"This is now bone of my bones
And flesh of my flesh;
She shall be called woman
For she was taken out of man."

For this reason a man will leave his father and mother and be united to his wife, and they will become one flesh.

The man and his wife were both naked, and they felt no shame.

Last Thursday, January 26, was an important day for me, not because of public events, but because it was the twenty-eighth anniversary of my first official date with Carey Stockman, now Carey Pollard, my wife. Not only was it our first date, it was also our first kiss: in the back seat of Gary Gulley's parents' blue Cadillac. It is funny how you remember details of certain events. We were sophomores in high school, and we had been interested in each other for about two months. The truth be told, Carey had been interested in me for longer than two months, but I was a bit slow in picking up on her signals. In other words, I was clueless. I loved to read books; I was worried about keeping my starting spot on the JV basketball team; and, frankly, I didn't quite understand girls. To give you a sense of how clueless I was, let me tell you how our relationship started. I should say that Carey has a slightly different version of this story, but she doesn't like to speak in public so you get to hear mine.

It was after a basketball game in November. Remember we were sophomores in high school, so, of course, there was only one person who was old enough to drive. He had his folks' station wagon and offered to take a group out for pizza. Carey came up to me and asked if I wanted to go. This is the key fact that Carey disputes: she says that I asked her but I know that I was much too confused by girls to have the guts to do such a thing. In any event, since there was only one driver, we ended up with nine or ten people piling into the station wagon. It was a time before everyone wore seat belts. Of course, this overcrowding meant that some of the girls had to sit on the laps of some of the boys. Carey worked it out so that she could sit on my lap, but I still did not pick up on the signal. The car was cramped so she had to rest her arm behind my head on my shoulder in order to sit on my lap. We were talking freely and I was having fun, but I still was not recognizing this as a special occasion. However, all of sudden, Carey was just not resting her arm behind my head; instead she started to play gently with the hair at the back of my neck. Even I noticed that, and I soon had a hard time breathing or speaking in complete sentences. Such is the power of touch—particularly touch as an expression of our sexuality.

There has been some discussion about sexuality over the last couple of weeks at JBU. And, while I appreciate the role of television news, newspapers, even the JBU online forums, I am not sure that they offer the best venues to talk about a subject as important and as complex as the Christian understanding of human sexuality. Indeed, I think chapel offers a more appropriate venue because Christians are called to understand truth in collective worship and we gather for worship in chapel. A good sermon seeks to embody truth, a goal that seems particularly important in thinking about sexuality. Moreover, while there has been a lot of talk of sexuality, there has not been, perhaps, enough talk of the biblical understanding of sexuality. As Christians, we are "people of the book." We are people who are committed to Scripture as the authority on how we should live our lives; a commitment that requires us to study and mediate on the Scripture so that the Holy Spirit can teach us truth. Accordingly, I think that it is right and fitting that we examine what Scripture has to say about sexuality and how we might gracefully call each other to follow that ideal at JBU.

I want to make a couple of assumptions to begin today, assumptions that may help to narrow what is a large topic. First, God clearly has created each one of us as a sexual person, by which I mean a person who has longings to be physically intimate with another human being. Second, while this longing for physical intimacy is an important part of our identity, it is not the most important part. If you hear nothing else from me to today, please hear this: you are first and foremost a beloved child of the living God whose deepest needs for intimacy can only be fully met in a relationship to him. If your core identity depends on physical intimacy with another human being, which is true of many in our world today, you will ultimately be disappointed and lost. Sex, even within marriage, cannot satisfy your deepest need to be loved—only Christ can meet that need.

Third, sexuality has a range of physical expression, everything from playing with the hair on the back of another person's neck to sexual intercourse. What are appropriate or inappropriate touches in particular contexts are important and difficult questions, but not the focus of my talk today. I want to begin by looking at sexuality as it is described in this passage in Genesis. That is sexuality in terms of physical intimacy which is ultimately expressed in intercourse—what the passage in Genesis describes as becoming one flesh. But it is also a physical intimacy that is clearly something prior to, and more than, just the act of intercourse— the physical intimacy that the passage describes as Adam and Eve being together naked and unashamed.

Scripture clearly teaches that this physical intimacy is reserved for the marriage relationship between a man and a woman. It is a doctrine that is rooted in creation as the passage in Genesis suggests when it offers the creation of Adam and Eve as the model for marriage: "for this reason [in other words, because of the model of creation] a man will leave his father and mother and be united to his wife, and they will become one flesh." It is a doctrine that is reaffirmed in the Gospels in Matthew 19:4-6: "haven't you read," Christ himself replies to his questioners, "that at the beginning the Creator 'made them male and female,' and said, 'For this reason a man will leave his father and mother and be united to his wife, and the two will become one flesh'? So they are no longer two, but one. Therefore what God has joined together, let man not separate." And the doctrine is reiterated again in Paul's letters. In these and other passages, Scripture affirmatively reserves physical intimacy for marriage between a man and a woman.

Scripture also specifically teaches that this physical intimacy is not appropriate in other relationships. Both in the Old and New Testament, Scripture asks us to avoid sexual immorality, which is defined as physical intimacy between a man and a woman who are not married to each other, or between a man and a man or a woman and a woman, or between adults and children, or between members of the same family, and the list goes on. Accordingly, Scripture consistently and repeatedly teaches that sexual physical intimacy should occur between a man and a woman who have covenanted to each other in the marriage relationship. That is the ideal that encourages us to flourish as human beings; that is the ideal that should shape our Christian lives and we should practice together; that is the ideal which we affirm at JBU.

But why? What is it about this level of physical intimacy that it should be expressed only in marriage? What is the purpose for physical intimacy? These are fair questions. Let me suggest that the purposes of sexual intimacy are fourfold. First, sex is, and continues to be for most people, the means by which we create babies. In other words, one of the purposes of sex is procreation. I recognize, of course, that modern technology has enabled us both to have sex without procreation and to have babies without sex. Questions of birth control and infertility are important, but again beyond the scope of my talk today. For today, it is important to recognize that procreation is one of the godly purposes of sex and that the scriptural ideal includes the conception, birth, and nurturing of a child within a family with a father and mother.

Second, one of the purposes of sex is pleasure, as it is expressed throughout the Song of Solomon, or as, say, in Proverbs 5:18-19: "may your fountain be blessed and may you rejoice in the wife of your youth. A loving doe, a graceful deer—may her breasts satisfy you always, may you ever be captivated by her love." The biblical ideal for sex recognizes that it can bring pleasure both to the man and to the woman and that pleasure is a good. Of course, it is this purpose that has been most warped by our contemporary culture. Sex is seen as only or primarily about pleasure, and pleasure is understood as the unequivocal and highest good. If sex brings pleasure, then it must be good. Moreover, any restrictions on pleasure are deemed morally wrong. This is the ethic of "hooking up," or "friends with benefits," or the "noncommittal make-out," all of which are single-minded pursuits of pleasure, to the exclusion of all other good purposes of physical intimacy. As Christians,

We also know, however, that we live in a fallen world in which God's ideals have been broken, bent, and warped. Perhaps even more difficult to acknowledge, we know that we ourselves are broken, bent, and warped. We are people who are sometimes unloving and selfish in our marriages. We are people who sometimes break our marriage vows to have affairs. We are people who sometimes cannot control our desire and have sex before marriage. We are people who sometimes fantasize about sex through pornography. We are people who sometimes lust with our eyes and in our hearts. We are people who sometimes engage in explicit sexual banter on the Internet. We are a people who sometimes dress to titillate. We are people who sometimes act out on our same-sex attraction. We have broken God's ideal for sexual intimacy in so many different ways. We are a people in need of repentance.

Even if we ourselves are not struggling right now to live out God's ideal of sexual intimacy, we are still falling short in helping others. We are a people who sometimes fail to confront friends when they begin to brag of a sexual exploit. We are a people who sometimes are afraid to help because we are worried about our own image. We are a people who do not often speak about this issue in church because it is impolite. We are a people sometimes afraid to talk with even our own children about sexual struggles because it may be too embarrassing. We are a people, and hear me on this one, who use the word "gay" as a general term of derision—that car is gay, that album is gay, that shirt is gay—not recognizing that the person next to us might be struggling with same-sex attraction and is now afraid to ask for help because of the hate that is heard in your voice. That is not right. We are also a people who excuse failures to live up to an ideal because we do not want to offend. That is also not right. We are a people who fail to love our neighbors who are struggling in this area. We are a people in need of repentance.

Of course, the magnificent thing about our faith is that Christ loves and forgives us. We serve a Christ who leaves the ninety-nine to find the one who is lost. We serve a Christ who hung out with sinners because it was not the healthy who needed a doctor, but the sick. We serve a Christ who forgives the woman caught in adultery but also tells her to go and sin no more. We serve a Christ who allows the prodigal son to take half his wealth and waste it in the distant country, but who also stands at the door waiting for him to return, waiting to welcome him back home as his son. We serve a Christ who calls us to live a righteous life but who also picks us up when we fail and turn to him.

And so should we at JBU. We should encourage each other to live out the biblical ideals to which we confess. When we fall short of the ideal, we should hold each other accountable in love to bring about repentance. We should extend grace to those who fall short; we should always hope and pray for restoration; and we should rejoice when restoration happens. Living out the Christian life is a messy business because we are all so broken in so many ways, but I believe that we are called to be a part of the messiness in people's lives because we are called to live out the principles of truth and grace in this world. It is what we should do at JBU.

I know that this ideal may be a hard word to hear and accept for those who are longing to be married, for those who are trapped in loveless marriages, for those who are struggling with same-sex attraction. It may seem to offer no hope for relationships that will be fulfilling, no opportunity for love, no compassion for their suffering. I do not offer this word lightly, but I do know that we serve a God of love, a God of hope, a God of compassion, and a God who understands our suffering. Take heart in the knowledge of God's character.

One final point: when Carey played with hair on my neck, she was picking me out for special attention. She was telling me through her touch that I was worthy of her affection, and she was selecting me out as the object of her love. That was twenty-eight years ago, and even through the ups and downs of life, I can testify to you that we continue to know each other better and to fall more deeply in love every year. The gift of a good marriage is a precious gift. However, it is not our most important gift. We both know that our love for Christ comes before our love for each other, that we are first beloved children of the living God before we are Mr. and Mrs. Pollard. That it is the touch of Christ's love that we need more than any touch from each other. May you also continue to find the touch of Christ's love the ground for your being and the hope for your salvation.

May it always be true of us.

Confession of a 500 Denarii Sinner

Text: Luke 7:36-50

Now one of the Pharisees invited Jesus to have dinner with him, so he went to the Pharisee's house and reclined at the table. When a woman who had lived a sinful life in that town learned that Jesus was eating at the Pharisee's house, she brought an alabaster jar of perfume, and as she stood behind him at his feet weeping, she began to wet his feet with her tears. Then she wiped them with her hair, kissed them and poured perfume on them.

When the Pharisee who had invited him saw this, he said to himself, "If this man were a prophet, he would know who is touching him and what kind of woman she is—that she is a sinner."

Jesus answered him, "Simon, I have something to tell you."

"Tell me, teacher," he said.

"Two men owed money to a certain moneylender. One owned him five hundred denarii, and the other fifty. Neither of them had the money to pay him back, so he canceled the debts of both. Now which of them will love him more?"

Simon replied, "I suppose the one who had the bigger debt canceled."

"You have judged correctly," Jesus said.

Then he turned to toward the woman and said to Simon, "Do you see this woman? I came into your house. You did not give me any water for my feet, but she wet my feet with her tears and wiped them with her hair. You did not give me a kiss, but this woman, from the time I entered, has not stopped kissing my feet. You did not put oil on my head, but she has poured perfume on my feet. Therefore, I tell you, her many sins have been forgiven—for she loved much. But he who has been forgiven little loves little."

Then Jesus said to her, "Your sins are forgiven."

The other guests began to say among themselves, "Who is this who even forgives sins?"

Jesus said to the woman, "Your faith has saved you; go in peace."

Our biblical text today tells a story of sin, forgiveness, and love. It tells, in other words, the good news of Jesus Christ, and it tells that story through the lives of two contrasting characters: Simon, a Pharisee and righteous leader in the community, and an anonymous woman who "lived a sinful life in that town." She is a woman without a name but with a reputation, a woman who was likely a prostitute, a woman that we might call today a whore or a slut—our harsh words for sinner. While she saw herself in the same terms, Christ saw her differently, which makes all the difference.

Consider the context of this dinner. It seems that Simon invites Jesus to dinner because he is interested about his teaching, not because he is a follower of it. The text says that they are "reclining" at the dinner, an indication that it was a more formal banquet in which the guests would lay on couches with their heads toward the center of the table and their feet toward the edge. Let me show you Nicolas Poussin's painting "Christ and the Adulteress" to give a sense of what the dinner might have looked like. This "reclining" at the table is significant for it explains why the woman anoints Jesus' feet instead of his head: his feet were more readily accessible to her.

The woman comes to the house because she too has heard about this teacher called Jesus. Commentators suggest that she was likely a disciple of John the Baptist and that she had probably already responded to John's message of repentance and forgiveness. And she was in deep need of forgiveness because of sin, not just her own sinful choices, but the weight of sin from a broken world. She was a prostitute. She gave her body to men in order to get money, and she knew that she was responsible for that action. However, she also lived in an economic system that was warped by sin and afforded women few choices to make money. Moreover, she could only make a living as a prostitute because there were men who were willing to pay her for sex, men whose disordered passions led them to desire sexual pleasure without the commitment of love. She both participated in sin and was the victim of it. She both chose wrongly and was wrongly chosen. She both sold a bent version of love for financial survival and was bent by the disordered love of others. Sin is both personal and structural, and it leaves us a mess. But she knew that she was a mess, so she was ready to hear and receive the good news, to hear that repentance will bring about forgiveness and restoration, to hear that no one is such a mess that God will not forgive them, to hear that this new teacher, this Jesus, was a "friend of sinners."

And so she takes the risk and comes to the house of the Pharisee, not knowing if she will be allowed in, but knowing the "look" that she will receive from the religious establishment if she is. She comes because she wants to thank Jesus for that good news. As she comes, she does not hide her status as a sinner. She brings an alabaster jar of perfume, a jar that she would have used to perfume herself and her home to prepare for her male customers. Prostitutes would also leave their faces unveiled and their hair down to signal to men their availability. She is unveiled and her long hair is readily available to dry the feet of Jesus. Indeed, she even begins to kiss the feet of Christ, a practice that some in the room may have interpreted as, again, part of her profession. She comes as she is, a sinner, not as she hopes to be; and she begins to cry.

As most of you know, crying is okay with me. In fact, I have heard rumors that some students have nicknamed me the crying president. No worries—I do not cry very often outside of chapel, nor am I on the verge of a nervous breakdown. Typically I am most often moved to tears in chapel when God speaks to me in truth and mercy, when I sense that God knows who I really am, with all of my pride, anger, and selfishness, yet still accepts me as his beloved child. I cry when I hear the good news and am deeply grateful that it is good news for me.

At the risk of reading myself into the text, I think that is why the woman is crying. Jesus knows the whole truth about her and her world—it is a mess—yet he still forgives and accepts her as his child. When she appears at the dinner, he does not give her a look of disdain. When she touches him, he does not recoil in judgment. And then, and this is a really amazing point, when Simon challenges Jesus claiming that he does not know that the woman who is touching him is a sinner, Jesus not only defends her, but also reinterprets everything she does as acts of worship rather than as the practices of a prostitute. Her tears and hair are not signals of her profession, but the water and towel to wash his feet. Her kissing of his feet is not to charm a customer, but to greet an important visitor. Her perfume is not to entice a stranger, but to anoint an honored guest. Jesus truly does know her and her love for him, so he sees her actions as gifts of devotion, not the practices of her sin. Looking at her through eyes of truth and mercy; Jesus no longer sees a prostitute—her many sins have been forgiven—he sees a beloved child of God. She has been forgiven much, so she loves much.

Simon, on the other hand, remains outside of the central drama of the story. He seems to invite Jesus to dinner out of curiosity rather than need. He is skeptical of the claims that Jesus is a prophet. He engages in verbal sparring with Christ, qualifying his responses like a debater: "I suppose the one who had the bigger debt canceled" would be the one who loves the most. He acts correctly with Jesus, but only correctly. In the social custom of the day, Simon was not required to wash his guests' feet, or greet them with a kiss, or anoint their heads with oil. You do those types of things only for guests that you really love and want to honor. He is a righteous person, a rigorous student of God's law, a religious leader. He sees himself as at least equal, if not superior, to Jesus. He does not see himself as needing much forgiveness, so he is certainly not going to cry, but nor is he going to love much. In his self-sufficiency, he remains outside this drama of the good news of Jesus.

Many of us too hang on to our self-sufficiency and righteous as the source of our identity. We do not see ourselves as 500 denarii sinners—those people go to the University of Arkansas; and we may not even see ourselves as fifty denarii sinners—they go to Oklahoma Baptist. But perhaps we should reflect again. We may not be prostitutes, but we are gossips. We may not be prostitutes, but we cannot control our anger. We may not be prostitutes, but we throw away more food than we eat. We may not be prostitutes, but we let a friend copy our homework. We may not be prostitutes, but we download pornography. We may not be prostitutes, but we avoid people who are weird or annoying or just different. We may not be prostitutes, but we each are a mess in our own individual ways. There are only 500 denarii sinners; the only question is whether we will recognize it and be willing to repent and be forgiven and made whole.

Now, this point came home to me in a new way over the Christmas break. Carey and I have been married for twenty-four years, and I have always considered myself a pretty good husband. I have remained faithful to her; I buy her flowers for no particular reason; I help with the dishes, although probably not enough; I bring her coffee in bed every morning; I encourage her strengths and sympathize with her struggles. I am not perfect by any means, but I have always seen my faults as a husband in the fifty denarii range. However, this past fall, I let her down. As some of you know, Carey's mom and brother both had cancer this fall. Her brother passed away in November, and her mother is slowly recovering. Both of them needed Carey a lot, and she spent a lot of time visiting them in Florida, on the telephone talking with them, and just thinking about them. She was doing the right thing, and I knew it, but, you see, I really am a 500 denarii sinner. I really am a mess and it started to show. I began to resent her being away from our family. I became angry about the telephone calls. I was jealous, not just for her time, but for her attention. My pride would assert its ugly head and I would remind her of our "important" work at the university or with the children at home. In short, I was more selfish than gracious, more needy than supportive, more demanding than patient, more uncaring than loving. I am a mess in my own particular way, and it was hurting the woman whom I love most.

Over the break, we had time away from the pressures of work and family, and I realized how much of a mess I had been. She too felt that the pressures of the fall had overwhelmed her perspective and her capacity to care for everyone. We talked, apologized, forgave, and renewed our love for one another. I needed much forgiveness in this situation, and love her more dearly for her willingness to grant it to me. Carey, thank you for your forgiveness and love.

Of course, my sin was not just toward Carey; my selfishness, anger, and jealousy revealed the mess that I am before God. I may not be a prostitute, but I can be deeply selfish. I may not be a prostitute, but I can be proud about my perceived importance. I may not be a prostitute, but I can even be jealous and angry about people who are sick. I am a mess before God, and I needed to confess my sin and hear again that he is willing to forgive me my sins and cleanse me from my unrighteousness.

So, JBU, let us come to the communion table as people who confess that we are a mess, each in our own individual ways, but who seek forgiveness: a people who can love much only because we have been forgiven much, a people who hear and receive the good news of Jesus Christ, the one who is the friend of sinners. And then we know that Christ will look at us through his truth and mercy, not seeing our mess, but seeing us as beloved children of the living God.

As a closing prayer, let me read for you a poem by George Herbert, a seventeenth-century Anglican priest. It is about Christ welcoming us sinners to his table.

Love (III)

Love bade me welcome, yet my soul drew back,
    Guilty of dust and sin.
But quick-eyed Love, observing me grow slack
    From my first entrance in,
Drew nearer to me, sweetly questioning
    If I lacked anything.

"A guest," I answered, "worthy to be here":
    Love said, "You shall be he."
"I, the unkind, ungrateful? Ah, my dear,
    I cannot look on thee."
Love took my hand, and smiling did reply,
    "Who made the eyes but I?"

"Truth, Lord; but I have marred them; let my shame
    Go where it doth deserve."
"And know you not," says Love, "who bore the blame?"
    "My dear, then I will serve."
"You must sit down," says Love, "and taste my meat,"
    So I did sit and eat.

May it always be true of us.

Christ Calls Us by Name

Text: John 10:1-6

"I tell you the truth, the man who does not enter the sheep pen by the gate, but climbs in by some other way, is a thief and a robber. The man who enters by the gate is the shepherd of his sheep. The watchman opens the gate for him, and the sheep listen to his voice. He calls his own sheep by name and leads them out. When he has brought out all his own, he goes on ahead of them, and his sheep follow him because they know his voice. But they will never follow a stranger; in fact, they will run away from him because they do not recognize a stranger's voice." Jesus used the figure of speech, but they did not understand what he was telling them.

Now I have to begin chapel today with a confession. I can't call all of you by name. It is painful for me to make this confession because I have met most of you, and you have introduced yourself to me, often on multiple occasions. I work hard at trying to remember names, printing out the pictures of my class or asking for help from Carey, but too often I fail to be able to recall the name in the moment of the conversation. Emily becomes Elizabeth, or Austin becomes Jackson, or Christa, Kristen, Crystal, Kirsten, or Christian: all become confused in my feeble brain. And sometimes, even when I remember the name, I don't pronounce it correctly. For instance, Lia. Lia was in my Gateway class last year, and she and Jose taught me a Guatemalan folk dance this past fall. Lia's real name, I think, is "A" "eu" "la" "lia"—which I had to spell out phonetically in this text and which I am sure that I still have gotten wrong. My thick tongue butchers the beauty of Spanish, or English for that matter. I have called Alyson Yawn-ichek, Alyson Jan-icheck for three years, even though her folks were on the parents' council. I try, I really do, to remember your names, but too often I fail. I am sorry. I sometimes even have to go through all four names of my children, Chadbenemmajames, to get to the right one.

You are all very generous in my struggle. When I am grasping for your name, you patiently introduce yourself again or you politely accept my mispronunciations as close enough. Moreover, almost all of you know my name, whether you call me Chip, Dr. Pollard, or President Pollard, so I always feel rude when I cannot remember yours. I also know that when I do get it right, it makes a difference. And that difference encourages me to keep trying, to keep entering into conversations hoping that the name will come to me, to keep finding ways to connect a name with a face. So, I trust that you will continue to be patient with me as we meet and I continue to try and call each of you by name.

My own failure to remember names has led me to understand this passage in a new way. We should understand the context of the passage first. Shepherding was a very common job throughout biblical times, so it is not surprising that Christ, as well as many other biblical writers, turn to shepherding as a useful metaphor for the Christian life. A shepherd would often be responsible for twenty to thirty sheep, and it was a common practice that four to five shepherds from the village would regularly keep their sheep in a common pen. This pen was typically a circle fenced by brambles and other sticks, and guarded by a watchman who literally slept at the gate which was the one opening in the circle. Indeed a similar system is still in place in many rural areas in two-thirds of the world today. I saw basically the same set-up in the Masai villages in Kenya this past summer. So the image here is a shepherd coming to the watchman at the open gate. The shepherd is not a thief that scrambles over the bramble; instead he is the person who has a right to gather up his own. He comes into the circle and calls out his twenty-five or so sheep from amongst maybe 150 sheep in the pen.

The sheep respond and follow him because he calls them by name and because they recognize his voice.

Now Scripture says that Jesus used this figure of speech, but the people did not understand him. In the Jewish context of the first century, there are several reasons that Christ's audience might not have understood. They were still unclear about Jesus' authority. They did not understand that he was Messiah, that he was coming to call his sheep, and that he was going to call both the Gentile and the Jew to be a part of the flock. They did not expect that God's kingdom would come through Messiah's sacrifice and death rather than through his political triumph. The remaining verses in chapter ten help to clarify those points to Christ's original audience. However, I wonder if we too have difficulty fully understanding the scope of this metaphor, this figure of speech, this portrait of Christ as our shepherd who calls us by name. Let me reflect on that with you for a few minutes.

Christ knows your name because he has chosen you. We choose the people that we name; we pick them out and we call them our own. Parents give children their legal names. I am Charles William Pollard, III, but my parents called me Chip. They gave me the legal name of my father and grandfather, but they also wanted to give me an independent name—Chip—which they said came from the "Ch" in Charles, the "i" in William and the "p" in Pollard. I am a bit skeptical of that etymology. Friends also give each other names. My friends growing up used to call me "Sequoia" because on the basketball court I was as tall and as quick as a tree. Lovers give each other names. When we were dating, I used to call Carey my Princess Adramine. I now have no idea why.

Christ knows our name, and the intimacy that suggests is quite staggering. Strangers do not know each by name, but Christ knows our names. And, Lord willing, we recognize his voice when he calls us by that name. Our identity, our security, our future is grounded in the fact that God knows our name and we respond to his voice. We are the beloved children of the living God, the sheep of his pasture. Now this truth does not somehow make us buddies with God. The sheep never assume that they are equal with the shepherd just because he calls them by name. However, our deepest longing for affirmation and intimacy is only met when we recognize the voice of the Christ who calls us by name. And we best recognize Christ's voice calling our name with his intimate affirmation by responding to him with praise and worship.

If Christ knows our name, he also knows our brokenness, our weaknesses, and even our failures. The shepherd does not quietly watch a sheep fall into the ditch. He calls the sheep by name to warn him of the danger. And, if the sheep is obstinate enough not to listen and to still fall into the ditch, the shepherd will come to help, correct, and comfort the wayward sheep. If you know someone's name, you can also call them to account. In class, as a few of you know from experience, I will often call on someone who looks like they are just about to fall asleep, but only if I know that person's name. And, if you are like me, your parents only used your full name when you had done something wrong. Whenever I heard my Dad going through the house looking for "Charles William Pollard the Third," I knew that I was in trouble. It is good that Christ knows our name well enough to speak into our brokenness, to call us to account for our failures, to challenge us to do more, or to counsel us to do less. Christ's love involves intimacy but it is also involves discipline. Christ calls us by name to offer words of correction, and we should recognize his voice in those words as well. We best recognize Christ's voice of correction by responding to it with confession, by recognizing our error, and turning in a new direction.

Christ calls us by name to affirm lovingly our identity in him, and we should respond with worship; he calls us by name to offer words of correction, and we should respond in confession. But most of the time he calls us by name just to follow him in the daily tasks of life, and we should respond in obedience. Sheep are dependent upon the shepherd for the stuff of ordinary life: for food, water, security, affection, for purpose and direction. If they don't obey, they die. Christ calls us by name so that we may faithfully follow him in the ordinary things of life: in doing our homework, caring for our roommate, encouraging our friends, welcoming the stranger, in giving to the poor, taking care of his creation, loving our families, relishing beauty, in being grateful, in praying for those who are hurting, in reading his Word.

I have seen Christ calling your name, and seen you following him in the ordinary things of life. I have heard about Bri who joined the Right Lead ministry at New Life Ranch to help needy children and only learned later when she showed up that the ministry involved horses, animals with which she had never worked before. I have heard Drew talk about getting up at 5:00 on Friday mornings to serve the basketball team as manager. I have read an essay by Kristen that showed a keen grasp, not only of the academic material, but also of how the material applied in the larger world. I have seen David and James and others lead an orientation program that helped to welcome the stranger to JBU. I read about Matt's work with homeless people at Genesis House.

Many of you recognize that the Christian life is lived, not primarily in the dramatic moments, but in the ordinary moments when we hear Christ call our name—when we recognize his voice and follow him. And, as it says in Psalm 23, sometimes he leads us to "green pastures" or "quiet waters" or in "paths of righteousness," but sometimes he leads us through the "valley of the shadow of death." In all of the different circumstances of life, we can affirm with David that "I will fear no evil, for you are with me; your rod and your staff, they comfort me. . . . My cup overflows. Surely goodness and love will follow me all the days of my life, and I will dwell in the house of the Lord forever" (Ps. 23:4-6).

So the next time your feeble-minded president forgets your name, you can smile and forgive him and say to yourself, "That's okay, Mr. President; you may have forgotten, but the King of Kings, the Lord of

Lords, the Alpha and Omega, the Wonderful Counselor, Mighty God, Everlasting Father, Prince of Peace, the one who was, who is, and who will always be—that God knows my name. He has chosen me from the beginning. He has blessed me with his love. He understands my brokenness. He holds me accountable for my error. He has asked me to follow him, and he has given me good things to do in his kingdom, not because he needs me, but because he loves me."

May it always be true of us.

CHAPTER 3

Advent at the University

The Incarnation Amidst Distractions

Advent at the university is always a time of strain. The students go home for Thanksgiving and return for the final two weeks of class and week of exams. If they have procrastinated on semester-long projects (and many of them do), they have lots of work to do to complete the research paper, deliver the presentation, or finish the portfolio. Even if they have not procrastinated, preparing for comprehensive final exams is enough to cause anyone a lot of anxiety. Moreover, the social calendar also accelerates in these final two weeks of class, with the annual Christmas dance and with each residence hall hosting Christmas parties on different nights, complete with elaborate decorations and food on each floor to welcome guests and to win competitions. The Cathedral Choir also performs its annual Christmas Candlelight service to three packed-out audiences during the final week of classes.

It is a bit daunting, then, to think about preparing an Advent sermon that might speak into this busyness and call students to reflect again on the coming of Christ as an infant. It is even more daunting because by the final week of class most of the students have met the expectation for chapel attendance, so they could readily find the press of papers and exams more urgent than yet another chapel service. Moreover, the students who need to go to the final chapel to meet their attendance requirement are often the same students who are struggling with procrastination in their academic work, so they can be fixated on those demands as they come to the service. In short, the audience is usually more distracted during this Advent service.

Of course, as I often tell students, college life is not just preparing for life; it is life, and the busyness and stress of the Advent season in the university mirrors, unfortunately, the situation of the world after college. Shopping for gifts, planning for church Christmas pageants, preparing rooms for out-of-town visitors, attending special holiday events and parties—the stress and strain of the Advent season has become a too common experience in all of our lives. Of course, Christ too was born in a time of stress and strain with everyone on the move to meet the requirements of the Roman census. It is in the midst of the busyness and distractions of life that we are called again and again to wonder at, and be grateful for, Christ's Incarnation.

A Light for Revelation

Text: Luke 2: 25-35

Now there was a man in Jerusalem called Simeon, who was righteous and devout. He was waiting for the consolation of Israel, and the Holy Spirit was upon him. It had been revealed to him by the Holy Spirit that he would not die before he had seen the Lord's Christ. Moved by the Spirit, he went into the temple courts. When the parents brought in the child Jesus to do for him what the custom of the Law required, Simeon took him in his arms and praised God saying:

"Sovereign Lord, as you promised, now dismiss your servant in peace. For my eyes have seen your salvation, which you have prepared in the sight of all people, a light for revelation to the Gentiles and for glory to your people Israel."

The child's father and mother marveled at what was said about him. Then Simeon blessed them and said to Mary, his mother: "This child is destined to cause the falling and rising of many in Israel, and to be a sign that will be spoken against, so that the thoughts of many hearts will be revealed. And a sword will pierce your own soul too."

I love Christmas trees, a real Fraser Fir, or a Blue Spruce which fills the room with a fragrant pine smell at the beginning of December and then fills the carpet with needles at the end of the month. As a young child, the purchase and decorating of the Christmas tree started the clock ticking toward Christmas morning and the opening of presents. As a high school student, I was dismayed to discover that my girlfriend, now my wife, Carey, had a fake tree in her family's home. It seemed sacrilegious. Her father was a cautious person, and he thought real trees were a fire hazard. Being a cocksure senior in high school,

I determined that it was time to introduce Carey and her family to the joys of a real tree. So I went out and purchased a tabletop tree and gave it to her as an early present for Christmas. How could her Dad refuse to allow her to accept a present? I am still amazed that he did not throw me out of the house. Several years later, I hid Carey's engagement ring as an ornament on one of those tabletop trees and watched with delight as she took over an hour to notice. A year later, we were married on December 17; we had a honeymoon for a week, and we moved into our new apartment on December 24. That apartment was furnished with a bed, a couch, and a Christmas tree that I had asked my brother to buy.

Of course, a person should be careful about what he gets started. My wife is now a Christmas tree nut. She has decorated five already this season, one with the students in the Walker Center, a large fake one in our home about which, I think, my father-in-law would smile, two small fake ones in Emma and James's rooms, and a real one with all of our family ornaments. Indeed, those ornaments record our family history in artifacts; it is sort of our family museum. For instance, we have an ornament that holds the ribbon from the box that held Carey's engagement ring. We have ornaments that mark the different places where we have lived in Boston or Oxford or Charlottesville or London. Each of the children has a box of the ornaments that they have made in school and at church—lots of glitter and macaroni on those. We even have some of my ornaments that I made as a child, not particularly beautiful, but Carey still remembers how much it meant to her when my mother gave her my childhood ornaments. But the most important thing on a Pollard Christmas trees is that it must have lights—many, many of them and they must all be white. We have over a thousand on one tree and eleven hundred on the other, and Carey continues to buy more strings. It is as if we are trying to illuminate the neighborhood from our bay window.

T. S. Eliot writes a series of poems for Advent, one of which he entitled "The Cultivation of Christmas Trees." In this poem, Eliot suggests that a child's approach to the Christmas tree offers us a model for how to view Christ's birth during the Advent season. He writes that for the child "the candle is a star, and the gilded angel / Spreading its wings at the summit of the tree / Is not only a decoration, but an angel. / The child wonders at the Christmas Tree." Wonder is that childlike attitude of expecting the miraculous in the ordinary, and wonder permeates the story of Christ's birth. It is hearing angels in a field, finding a king in a manger, and following a star to a Savior. It is the experience that involves joy and fear, elation and terror.

Eliot goes on to suggest that we need to cultivate that spirit of wonder as a habit of being because it is so easy to become cynical or discouraged. He writes a benediction for the child who will grow to adulthood in this weary world: "Let him continue in the spirit of wonder . . . So that the reverence and the gaiety / May not be forgotten in later experience / In the bored habituation, the fatigue, the tedium, / The awareness of death, the consciousness of failure." I have to admit that it has become more and more difficult for me to cultivate that wonder during the Advent season as I have grown older. Advent can easily become more about obligation—the purchase of gifts, the writing of cards, and the attending of parties—than about expectation, more about busyness than about awe.

Eliot suggests that if we can continue to cultivate that wonder year in and year out, we deepen our experience of the reverence and the gaiety of Christ's birth. The accumulated memories of annual emotion concentrate the experience into a habit. This habit of wonder is a great joy because Christ's birth offers salvation. It is also a great fear because Christ makes his claim on our whole life. His birth brings hope, but it also brings judgment. His first coming foretells his second. Wonder consists precisely in cultivating this twofold sense of joy and fear, gaiety and reverence, celebration and deference.

In the Gospel of Luke, we have an example of a person—Simeon—who had developed that habit of wonder. He may well also have been a person who had reached his eightieth year.

I want to make just a couple of observations about Simeon that may help us develop this habit of wonder. He knows how to wait. He was waiting for the consolation of Israel, which was a way to say that he was waiting for Christ's first coming. During that time of waiting, he lived a righteous and devout life and was sensitive to the leading of the Holy Spirit. Luke mentions three times that the Holy Spirit was upon, moved, or was revealed to Simeon. We are in an analogous position; we are waiting for Christ's second coming and we are equally called to live righteous and devout lives and to be sensitive to the Holy Spirit. Wonder develops out of the rituals of righteousness and devotion and the promptings of the Holy Spirit.

Simeon also knows of the joy and seriousness of waiting for Christ. He knows that when he sees Christ, then he will die. He also knows that Christ will be a controversial figure, causing the rising and falling of many, and that his life will even cause sorrow to his mother. Simeon's habit of wonder is not Pollyannaish or naïve. It is a wonder that recognizes the joy and fear of Christ's presence, and yet it still finds peace in that presence.

Finally, Simeon conveys his sense of wonder of Christ through words of poetry and song, words that have been put to music by the church for generations: "Sovereign Lord, as you have promised, now dismiss your servant in peace. For my eyes have seen your salvation, which you have prepared in the sight of all people, a light for revelation to the Gentiles and for glory to your people Israel." It is a fantastic picture of wonder: an old man who waited his whole life for this moment holds the baby who will bring about the salvation for all people. Simeon turns to metaphors of illumination to convey his wonder of the Christ child; he is "a light for revelation to the Gentiles and for glory to your people Israel."

Christ's presence in our lives as light and glory, luminosity and radiance, shining and brilliance, and our response as one of wonder and worship. In this candlelight service, we also have the privilege now at the end of this service to represent to each other how the light of God's salvation has been prepared in the sight of all people. As these ordinary bits of candle wax enable us to share the miraculous light of fire, so also in our ordinary human lives, we should testify to our God's saving light. Let us pass the light of Christ to one another and respond with praise and wonder at the one who is "light for revelation to the Gentiles and for glory to your people Israel."

May it always be true of us.

Go Home by Another Way:
Adoration of the Magi

Text: Matthew 2:1-12

After Jesus was born at Bethlehem in Judea during the time of King Herod, Magi from the east came to Jerusalem and asked, "Where is the one who has been born king of the Jews? We saw his star in the east and have come to worship him."

When King Herod heard this he was disturbed, and all Jerusalem with him. When he had called together all the people's chief priests and teachers of the law, he asked them where the Christ was to be born. "In Bethlehem in Judea" they replied, "for this is what the prophet has written:

"But you, Bethlehem, in the land of Judah, are by no means the least among the rulers of Judah; for out of you will come a ruler who will be the shepherd of my people Israel."

Then Herod called the Magi secretly and found out from them the exact time the star had appeared. He sent them to Bethlehem and said, "Go and make a careful search for the child. As soon as you find him, report to me, so that I too may go and worship him."

After they heard the king, they went on their way, and the star they had seen in the east went ahead of them until it stopped over the place where the child was. When they saw the star, they were overjoyed. On coming to the house, they saw the child with his mother Mary, and they bowed down and worshipped him. Then they opened their treasures and presented him with gifts of gold and of incense and of myrrh. And having been warned in a dream not to go back to Herod, they returned to their country by another route.

We are going to begin today with an abbreviated Sunday school Christmas pageant. Many of you probably have participated in these annual church rituals or at least have seen the Charlie Brown version on television. Perhaps some of you women harbored secret hopes to be picked as Mary so that you could carry a doll onto the church stage, and probably some of you men just wanted to be a donkey or some other animal so that you didn't have to learn any lines. We only have time to act out the scene with the Magi, and I will serve as narrator to fill in a bit of the historical context.

Matthew never specifies the number of Magi in his account, but since the second or third century the church has typically identified three people, carrying the three gifts, so we have three in our pageant this morning. The church fathers developed quite a tradition around these three men. Augustine gave the Magi the names Balthassar, Melchior, and Caspar. Irenaeus speculated on the significance of their gifts, claiming that the gold represented Christ's role as King because it was so costly, the frankincense represented Christ's deity because it was the incense burned on pagan altars, and the myrrh represented Christ's death because it was used to prepare dead bodies. Our wise men are also bringing gold (or least a facsimile of gold), frankincense, and myrrh today. Finally, the Venerable Bede, the English monk of the seventh century, reported that the Magi came from Asia, Africa, and Europe as a way to suggest that they represented the ends of the known world.

While the church has developed these traditions, Scripture gives us only a few facts: some unknown number of Magi see a strange star and follow it. They come to Jerusalem and inquire of Herod about the birth of a new king. After consulting his advisors, Herod tells them that the king will be born in Bethlehem and asks them to search for this new king and report back to him. The Magi follow the star to that village, come and find Mary and Jesus, bow down and worship him, and then they give him expensive gifts of gold, frankincense, and myrrh. Finally, they are warned in a dream not to go to Herod but to go home by another way.

It is interesting to speculate why the church developed such a rich tradition about the Magi. Compare them, for instance, with the shepherds who are also unnamed and unnumbered in Scripture but around which comparatively little extra-biblical lore has developed. Let me suggest a few reasons that may help us think about the importance of the Magi to us today.

The visit of the Magi suggests that Christ's birth has significance far beyond a little town in Bethlehem or the small religion of Judaism. Indeed, in the Western branch of the church, we celebrate the visit of the Magi on January 6, during the Feast of the Epiphany. Epiphany means manifestation or showing or appearance, and what the church is celebrating on this feast day is that Christ is revealing himself to the Gentiles, that his message is not only for the Jews but also for the whole world.

Again, it is useful to compare Luke's account of the shepherds and Matthew's account of the Magi to see this point. The shepherds are simple people, engaged in rural, subsistence agriculture. They are probably poor, certainly Jewish, and they have no gifts to offer. When you finish Luke's account of the birth of Christ, you recognize that this child very well could be the Messiah of the Jewish people. The angels offer plenty of evidence for Christ's deity, but his relevancy to the rest of the world is still not clear. Even though the angels say that this baby will be "good news of great joy for all the people," the birth of Christ as recorded in Luke is a still a local, rural, and very Jewish event.

The visit of the Magi in Matthew radically changes the earthly scope of Christ's birth because now even the pagan world is coming to pay homage to this child. The Magi's visit suggests that Christ will be the savior not just of the Jews, but of the whole world. While the shepherds are simple farmers, the Magi are scholars. The shepherds are poor and live out in fields, while the Magi are rich and probably came from a large city. The shepherds are of the peasant class, the Magi have access to kings and may even have been kings themselves. The visit of the Magi suggests that Christ's birth cuts across all economic, social, ethnic, and religious identities—that he deserves the worship and praise of all people.

So, we can begin to see why the early church, which we must remember had far more Gentile than Jewish converts, might be interested in these Magi who were smart, rich, and Gentile. The Magi represent their place in the story of Christ's birth. What about us? Aren't we much closer to the Magi than to any other of the characters in the story of Christ's birth? By just being here at JBU, aren't we people who, at least in a world context, are scholars, wealthy, upper-class, and certainly Gentile? Shouldn't the Feast of the Epiphany be central to our lives because it celebrates Christ's including us in his salvation story? I would like to suggest that we should see ourselves in terms of the Magi as we approach this Advent season. We should imagine their journey to the Christ child as an example for what our journey should be this season. So, let's look again at their journey from that perspective.

"We saw his star in the east and have come to worship him."

Consider what prompted their journey. They see an unusual star in the heavens. The Magi are wise men, scholars, and the scholarship of the day often involved a study of the stars—astrology. But this new star must have been quite something to prompt them to journey toward it, for traveling was neither easy nor cheap in the first century. The Magi likely traveled in caravans with hired men or slaves, and with the constant risk of bandits, sickness, or injury on the journey. Journeys could last months, even years. There were no rest areas or Holiday Inns along the way. Not only was there risk to their physical well-being, but also risk to their reputations. Remember that the Magi were likely people who had wealth, prestige, social status, family, and work. They were giving up a lot to follow a star, even if it gave evidence of the birth of the King of the Jews. In fact, Israel was a minor nation which was subjected to the rule of Rome. Even if the promise of the star was true, why bother for this small nation? They must have looked very foolish to their friends and family as they departed, and they probably had self-doubt themselves about the wisdom of their journey. Even so, they followed their curiosity to find the promise of this star and this King.

Our journey to Christ may seem equally foolish to some. Religion is the opium of the masses, says Marx, not the wisdom of the intellectuals or the powerful or the rich. Governmental agencies promise to meet the needs of others more effectively than the church. The advertising of consumer goods holds out the promise of more happiness than religious faith. Yet, we still have our stars that prompt and lead us to Christ. It may be the deep ache of loneliness even in a busy life; it may be the longing for coherence in a world of fragmentation; it may be keen curiosity about the purpose of life. God set stars in our lives, and it is okay to follow them even if we appear foolish. In fact, such foolishness is often a defining part of the Christian life.

However, as the Magi leave their homes, they are still operating in the world that they know, the world of worldly power and prestige. So, when they come first to Jerusalem, the center of power in Israel, they seek out King Herod. Again you must wonder about the wisdom of this move. They come to King Herod and ask to worship the new king of his country. Of course, King Herod was disturbed. These Magi were telling him that he had a rival, that his family was no longer going to rule, and that his power was at risk. Indeed, it tells us something about the high social status of these Magi that they could get to see King Herod in the first place and that King Herod didn't kill them immediately when they told him their story. In their foolishness, they speak the truth to power, a lesson for us all.

"But you, Bethlehem, in the land of Judah, are by no means the least among the rulers of Judah."

Indeed, as Scripture gives evidence time and time again, God tends not to work through the normal channels of power. He works with Israel, not with Rome. Christ is born in Bethlehem, not in Jerusalem. He is born to an unwed mother, not to the king of the country. Like the Magi, we too must be open to having our normal expectations changed about where Christ will be found. We must be willing to follow the star even if it leads to Bethlehem, the place that seems insignificant in our eyes but that is also the place where Christ is waiting for us to worship him.

This Christmas season might be a good time to reflect on what might be your next Bethlehem, the next place that you will meet Christ. We come to the university with dreams about majors, careers, spouses, and friends. We also come with fears of failure, of looking foolish, of being alone. Some of you may worry that you need to be all grown up by the time you finish here at JBU: that you must have a promising career, a loving spouse, a coherent set of beliefs, and a faithful set of friends before graduation. In other words, like the Magi, we tend to look for Christ in the normal places that our culture, even our Christian culture, tells us that we find happiness and success. However, as the story of the Magi shows, Christ is more often found in the most unusual places.

Let me give you one example from my life. As some of you may remember, I practiced law for a while with a firm called Latham & Watkins in Chicago. It was a big firm with over eight hundred lawyers across the country. Our clients included corporations such as Citicorp, Marriott, and Sears. In fact, the office was in the Sears Tower in Chicago on the fifty-eighth floor. In terms of our normal cultural expectations, Latham & Watkins was a place of great success, wealth, and power.

On my first day at the job, I met the lawyer in the office next to mine. He had a Focus on the Family coffee mug on his desk, so I wondered if he might be a believer. However, when we talked, there was not a lot of overt evidence of his faith. Over the next year I worked with him on several cases. He worked very hard; indeed, one year he billed time for all but twenty-five days of the year, including Saturdays and Sundays. I didn't spend as much time as he did in the office, but I was diligent in my work and I earned his trust. I found out that his wife had gone to Liberty University (it was her coffee cup on his desk) and that he had grown up in the Lutheran church. They were not going to church then, however, even though his wife was urging them to visit. We grew to be good friends, eating lunch together often and riding the train home. On one occasion, we were talking about church on the ride home, and he was listing all of the problems with the churches that they had visited. He talked about all of the hypocrisy of members in those churches, and all of the difficulties of his schedule to find time to go to church. I finally stopped him, and simply said, "You should go to church. None of them are perfect. Just pick one and go. It will be good for your marriage, for your family, and for you." He was taken aback by my abruptness, but he listened and started going to church, and it was true—it was good for his marriage, for his family, and for him.

About a year to a year-and-a-half later, Carey and I were at their house. It was a farewell party for us. After three years at the firm, I was leaving to go back to graduate school to go into teaching. My friend and his wife had become active in a local church and their spiritual life was thriving. At the dinner, I recalled the conversation in the train, and my friend's wife smiled and said, "Chip, what you don't know is that I had been praying for about two years before you came to the firm that someone would come into my husband's life and encourage him in his faith. I think that you were the answer to that prayer."

Now, I must admit such talk makes me nervous, not only because I am wary of taking credit for being God's instrument, but even more so because it says something that I think is true about God's economy. You see, in God's economy perhaps the main purpose of all my work in law school and at the firm was to establish a relationship with my friend so that God could encourage him in his faith. God's economy sometimes scares me because it was not at all how I judged my success as a lawyer. I thought in terms of successful negotiations and year-end bonuses. All of that work seemed foolish to me if the true purpose was just to develop this one relationship, but we should remember that we serve the God who leaves the ninety-nine to find the one. God's economy is also what we see in the story of the Magi: scholars, who may well be kings, who have been trained in the best science of the day, and who have great riches, risk everything to go to worship a baby. This baby was not even in Jerusalem, but in Bethlehem.

Your Bethlehem may be an AIDS clinic in Kenya or a public school in Kansas. It may be in graduate school studying political science or at home taking care of a sick relative. It may be building houses in the city or designing advertising for corporations. No matter where God calls us to worship him through the work of our lives, we must come prepared to use our gifts and lavish them upon him in worship and praise. The Magi come to Bethlehem. They bow down and worship the Christ child and then open their treasures and give him their gifts. We too are asked to give him our gifts in whatever context he calls us to serve.

"They returned to their country by another route."

There is one final point of the story. In a dream, the Magi receive a warning and are told to go home by another way. They do not return to Herod; they do not return to their normal expectations of power; indeed, they probably do not return home the same people. They are changed by their experience with Christ, and they go home by a different route. T. S. Eliot writes a poem, "The Journey of the Magi," in which he tries to express the fundamental change that happens in a person who has come into the true presence of Christ. He writes in the voice of one of the Magi who is now old and retells the story of their trip to see Christ. This elderly Magi says, "I had seen birth and death / But had thought they were different; this Birth was / Hard and bitter agony for us, like Death, our death." Eliot is following the familiar scriptural truth that our new birth in Christ means a death of our self, and that death is difficult. It is a difficult truth for the Magi, for they are people with intelligence, wealth, social status, and achievement. They have a lot of self to give up, and so do we. The Magi are people, in other words, who benefit from the expectations of their culture, and so are we. We love the mall. We fill the Advent season with parties. We are inundated by advertisements for things that lure us with happiness; and we spend and spend and spend our time, money, and energy on chasing the cultural ideal of Christmas, an ideal that we can never obtain and that will never satisfy us. Instead, we should follow the lead of Eliot's Magi, who are "no longer at ease here, in the old dispensation, / With an alien people clutching their gods."

Let us be uneasy this Advent season because we have met the true Christ. Let us be uneasy so that we will not become so quickly caught up in the cultural expectations of our world. Let us be uneasy with an alien people clutching their gods of Christmas hype and consumerism. Let us be uneasy so that we may find Christ in our Bethlehem. Let us be uneasy so that we might be willing to be foolish. And let us be uneasy so that we might find a new way to go home, a new way to be in this world this Advent season.

May it always be true of us.

Let It Be to Me

Text: Luke 1:26-55

In the sixth month, God sent the angel Gabriel to Nazareth, a town in Galilee, to a virgin pledged to be married to a man named Joseph, a descendant of David. The virgin's name was Mary. The angel went to her and said, "Greetings, you who are highly favored! The Lord is with you."

Mary was greatly troubled at his words and wondered what kind of greeting this might be. But the angel said to her, "Do not be afraid, Mary, you have found favor with God. You will be with child and give birth to a son, and you are to give him the name Jesus. He will be great and will be called the Son of the Most High. The Lord God will give him the throne of his father David, and he will reign over the house of Jacob forever; his kingdom will never end."

"How will this be," Mary asked the angel, "since I am a virgin?"

The angel answered, "The Holy Spirit will come upon you, and the power of the Most High will overshadow you. So the holy one to be born will be called the Son of God. Even Elizabeth your relative is going to have a child in her old age, and she who was said to be barren is in her sixth month. For nothing is impossible with God."

"I am the Lord's servant," Mary answered. "May it be to me as you have said." Then the angel left her.

At that time Mary got ready and hurried to a town in the hill country of Judea, where she entered Zechariah's home and greeted Elizabeth. When Elizabeth heard Mary's greeting, the baby leaped in her womb, and Elizabeth was filled with the Holy Spirit. In a loud voice she exclaimed: "Blessed are you among women, and blessed is the child you will bear! But why am I so favored, that the mother of my Lord should come to me? As soon as the sound of your greeting reached my ears, the baby in my womb leaped for joy. Blessed is she who has believed that what the Lord has said to her will be accomplished!"

And Mary said:

"My soul glorifies the Lord and my spirit rejoices in God my Savior,
for he has been mindful of the humble state of his servant.
From now on all generations will call me blessed,
for the Mighty One has done great things for me—holy is his name.
His mercy extends to those who fear him, from generation to
generation.
He has performed mighty deeds with his arm;
he has scattered those who are proud in their inmost thoughts.
He has brought down rulers from their thrones but has lifted up
the humble.
He has filled the hungry with good things but has sent the rich
away empty.
He has helped his servant Israel, remembering to be merciful to
Abraham and his descendants forever, even as he said to our
fathers."

Now, in my Protestant upbringing, we never heard much about Mary, other than I knew that she was the prize role to play in the church Christmas pageant for any second- or third-grade girl. However, amongst Protestants and others, there is a resurgent interest in Mary and her role, not only in the narrative of Christ's birth, but also an example of how to live our lives. In fact, even as I was preparing this sermon, I received this month's copy of *Christianity Today*, which has a picture of Mary on the cover and a lead article on her by Scot McKnight, the professor from North Park University who spoke in chapel earlier in November. We are in good company thinking about Mary today.

"Greetings, you who are highly favored! The Lord is with you."

We should begin with the annunciation, that is with the announcement by Gabriel to Mary that she has found favor with God, that the Lord is with her. She will give birth to the "Son of the Most High," who will "have the throne of his father David and will reign over the house of Jacob forever; his kingdom will never end." In a classic understatement, the text says that Mary was troubled by Gabriel's words and even questions his understanding of biology: "How will this be since I am a virgin?" Surely we can understand her position. She is young, probably fourteen to sixteen. She is a virgin, a fact that is repeated three times for emphasis in the text; and she is engaged to be married, which, in her culture, was as serious as being married. Gabriel comes and announces to Mary that she has found favor with God, an announcement which means she will be an unwed mother who will likely be disgraced and divorced and who will live out her life in poverty and shame, if she and her child are allowed to live at all. If that is the favor of God, you can understand why Mary might be a bit troubled and incredulous.

Why does God show his favor on Mary, this young, unwed virgin, to be the mother of his son? Let me offer three suggestions for possible reasons. First, God establishes an important theological truth by having Christ born of the virgin, Mary. It is the truth of the Incarnation that Jesus was both fully God and fully human. As it says in the Apostles' Creed, Christ was conceived by the Holy Spirit and born of the Virgin Mary—fully God and fully human. The Incarnation is a mystery as great as the virgin birth that produced it, yet it is a doctrine that is at the center of our faith. Christ understands and is sympathetic to our human frailty because he is fully human, but Christ can bring about our redemption because he is fully God.

Even so, if I were Mary, I am not sure I would like God making important theological points at the expense of my reputation. I would certainly not call it his favor. You can just imagine how the people of Nazareth, people who were really not much different than us, must have talked about Mary and the birth of this seemingly illegitimate first child. They would likely remind each other of the unfortunate timing of the birth, "Well, you know that Jesus was born before they got married?" or "Do you remember when Mary went away to her cousins while she was pregnant?" Or, the famous backhanded compliment, "Haven't they done well to make such a good thing out of a bad start?" I imagine that Mary, and by extension, Jesus, had a "reputation" even though neither one deserved it.

We know what it means to have a "reputation," don't we? Let me tell you a brief story about "reputations" in my family, a story that Carey has given me permission to tell. As you know if you have been around here at JBU, Carey and I started dating when we were sophomores in high school. I had been interested in her for a couple of months before I told my family. I was worried that it would not work out or that I would look foolish, so I did not tell anyone. When I finally told my mother and sister that I was "going with" Carey, my sister's first response was, "Well, you know that she has a reputation." Ouch—that one hurts to hear from your older sister about your new girlfriend. It was true that Carey had made some bad choices in middle school and beginning of high school. It was also true that she had decided to break with that past and renew her commitment to Christ. She even asked God to bring a good Christian guy into her life, and then who should arrive on the scene but me—what providential timing. However, Carey's "reputation" still lingered in the mind of my sister, and she was just trying to protect her little brother from being tainted by that reputation. Of course, what neither my sister nor I were willing to recognize was that we too had "reputations," even if those reputations were defined by more socially acceptable sins such as pride, gossip, selfishness, and avarice. We all have "reputations"—it is part of what it means to be sinners—but some reputations seem to carry a darker stain than others, and being an unwed mother or illegitimate child seems to be one of those.

Second, it is interesting, I think, that in his providence, God had Christ grow up in a family that would have been talked about as having a reputation, even though it was undeserved. I wonder if it made him more open as an adult to hanging out with all of those people who had reputations—the tax collectors, the prostitutes, the money lenders, the adulterers. He understood that these men and women of reputation were first children of God and that even though they might have been stained by their choices, they remained of ultimate value because they were made in the image of God. Christ knew how to encourage rather than to judge people with reputations to live a righteous life. As he says to the woman caught in adultery, "Neither do I condemn you. Go now and leave your life of sin" (John 8:11). He talks with sinners, not about them, and in the process he seeks to bring about their redemption. We should do likewise.

A third possible reason for choosing the virgin Mary was so God could show his power. God often picks the weak, the barren, the poor, the fragile to do his work so that it will be clear that it is God who is doing the work, not us. Moses couldn't speak; Sarah and Hannah were barren; David was the youngest child in his family; Ruth was a widow; Daniel a refugee; and Mary was a teenage virgin. God choose the virgin Mary to have his child because it shows, as Gabriel says, that "nothing is impossible with God." Indeed, the virgin birth itself gives us great hope because it reminds us that "nothing is impossible with God." If God can enable a virgin to give birth to his son, then he can bring about peace between the warring factions in the Middle East. He can bring life to the millions of hungry people, provide jobs for those out of work, bring about reconciliation in your parents' marriage, make a way for you to pay next semester's bill, and he can bring friends to comfort the lonely. For "nothing is impossible with God."

"I am the Lord's servant. May it be to me as you have said."

So how do we respond to the expression of God's power? How does Mary respond to God's announcement through Gabriel? "I am the Lord's servant. May it be to me as you have said." She begins with a declaration of her position vis-à-vis God. She is the Lord's servant; she is not in charge. It reminds me of a key passage in Shakespeare's *King Lear*. Lear's servant, Kent, tells him the truth that he is foolish to split up his kingdom and give it to his daughters. For speaking this uncomfortable truth, Kent is banished, under the threat of death, from Lear's kingdom. Even with this threat, Kent remains faithful to Lear and returns in disguise so that he can continue to be Lear's servant. When Lear meets the disguised Kent, he asks Kent why he wants to serve him. Kent replies: "You have that in your countenance which I would fain call master." Lear asks, "What's that?" and Kent answers, "Authority." Mary is willing to be God's servant because she recognizes his authority; it is a part of his character. She is willing to risk divorce, disgrace, poverty, perhaps even death for her child and herself, because she trusts God's authority to have claim over her life. She says to him, "May it be to me as you have said." May it be, the Latin phrase for which is "*fiat*," a word that we usually associate with a command, but that here is the obedient acceptance of God's command. The flip side of God's power is Mary's *fiat*. I will serve the King because he is the King. God may do the impossible, but he may do it through us. Are we willing for him to do so? Are we willing to risk our reputations, our relationships, our riches, our health, even our lives to be the Lord's servant? Are we willing to be "favored" of God?

Sometimes the impossible involves the mundane. Are you willing to study in college for four years, medical school for four years, internship and residence for three, and fellowship for four to be a doctor through whom God can do the impossible? Sometimes the impossible involves small actions. Are you willing to pray for and visit a friend suffering from depression? Sometimes the impossible involves others. Are you willing to move your family to a different part of the country to be God's servant? Sometimes the impossible involves simply trusting, in life and in death, that the baby is the King and that the King knows what he is doing.

"My soul glorifies the Lord and my spirit rejoices in God my Savior."

Mary does not merely respond to this news by submitting herself to God's authority, she also worships God for having chosen her. When Mary visits Elizabeth and receives confirmation of Gabriel's message, Mary breaks out into song: "My soul doth magnify the Lord and my spirit hath rejoiced in God my Savior." The church has historically called this song the Magnificat because it magnifies or praises the greatness of God. It is about the God who chooses the adolescent virgin to do his work because he is great, and the God who is merciful to those who fear him because he is great. It is about the God who scatters the proud, who brings down the rulers, and who lifts the humble because he is great. It is about the God who fills the hungry with good food because he is great. It is about the God who keeps his promises forever because he is great, and a God who calls us to do the impossible because he is great. It is about God, for he is great.

Mary's song calls us to bring together orthodoxy and orthopraxis, right thinking and right living, in our spiritual lives. Too often in the church we are asked to emphasize one or the other—the truth or social action, the Bible or taking care of the poor. However, Mary holds together both. She is a young girl who is steeped in the Scriptures; within the nine verses of her hymn lie about fifteen identifiable Old Testament quotations. She cares about the truth of Scripture and about thinking through Scripture to determine who God is and what he wants us to do. She knows that God is her savior and that his name is holy, but she also finds in Scripture what we all should find in Scripture: that God cares about people, particularly people who are suffering from hunger or sickness or poverty or injustice or loneliness. And God asks us to do the impossible and care for each other in our suffering. He calls us to the impossible tasks of feeding the hungry, responding to the poor, caring for the sick and dying, and seeking justice for the oppressed. He calls us to live righteous lives. In this song, Mary shows how she aspires to think right and live right. In this Advent season, let us follow Mary's example and worship the Christ in both thought and deed, in praise and service, in word and action.

I know that some of you are already following Mary's example. Professor Joe Walenciak's Gateway class is raising money to offer a Christmas celebration to four hundred children in Guatemala City, and Professor Carli Conklin's Gateway class will be sending presents to thirteen children whose fathers are in prison. Thank you for being willing to serve the King and for believing that "nothing is impossible with God."

"Nothing is impossible with God."

Again, if you have been around at JBU, you know that when I preach, I tend to be preaching as much to myself as to anyone else. I have to tell you today that Mary's story is a pretty important one for me and my family during this Advent season, as Carey's brother is sick. He has cancer and the prognosis is not good, but we are clinging to the hope that "nothing is impossible with God." If God can give birth to his son through a virgin, then he certainly can heal the sick, even the dying; and, even if the worst should come, Mary's story gives us hope because we know that her baby, the Son of God born of a virgin, went on to conquer death. It is why it is fitting today that we will end this reflection on Christ's birth with a communion service that celebrates his death and resurrection. Christ was born to die so that we might have life. Christmas always points toward Good Friday and Easter. We can truly say that "nothing is impossible with God" because we believe that Christ has risen from the dead and will raise us from the dead.

Now my brother-in-law has also helped me to understand Mary's response to God's power and authority, for he too has found a way to respond to troubling, even impossible, news by saying, "May it be to me as you have said." Let me just read to you a couple of lines from his latest email.

130

God has a plan for my life, and I am thinking it may be to annoy as many different nurses as possible . . . . I sincerely believe God is in control and His plan is best for not only me but everyone I come in contact with. Since I believe that, being sick or well truly is not the point; the only thing that matters is trying to do His will.

His words seem to me another way to say to our mighty God, "I am the Lord's servant. May it be to me as you have said."

As you come to the communion table, may I ask a favor? Could you pray for my brother-in-law, and for one other person or situation that seems to be impossible? And, as you go through this Advent season, remember with me that "nothing is impossible with God." Remember that our response to his power and authority is willing acceptance, "May it be to me as you have said," and praise, "my soul doth magnify the Lord and my spirit rejoices in God my Savior."

May it always be true of us.

---

*My brother-in-law, Timothy Wade Stockman, died eleven months after I originally gave this presentation. He was forty years old. And yet, even more so in death, his words ring true: "being sick or well truly is not the point; the only thing that matters is trying to do His will." We find comfort in Mary's song, "My soul glorifies the Lord and my spirit rejoices in God my Savior."

We Are the Subplot

Text: Luke 3:4-6, 15-16

As it is written in the book of the words of Isaiah the prophet:

"A voice of one calling in the desert: 'Prepare the way for the Lord, make straight paths for him. Every valley shall be filled in, every mountain and hill made low. The crooked roads shall become straight, the rough ways smooth. And all mankind will see God's salvation.". . .

The people were waiting expectantly and were all wondering in their hearts if John might possibly be the Christ. John answered them all, "I baptize you with water. But one more powerful than I will come, the thongs of whose sandals I am not worthy to untie. He will baptize you with the Holy Spirit and with fire."

The passage for today should be a familiar one. It is the prophecy in Isaiah about John the Baptist, the son of Zechariah and Elizabeth, the relative of Christ, and the one who is called to prepare the way for Christ. Zechariah, Elizabeth, and John do not often make it into our Christmas dramas or pageants at church during the Advent season. Perhaps it is because parents would rather their daughters be beautiful angels than the old, barren Elizabeth, or would rather their sons be shepherds or wise men rather than the old, mute Zechariah. In other words, we rarely see Zechariah, Elizabeth, and John in our Christmas pageants because they are clearly supporting characters rather than the stars of the Christmas story. Indeed, their family is the subplot in the Christmas narrative, the people whose actions, dialogue, and responses comment on the main plot of Mary, Joseph, and Jesus.

As you may already know from Masterpieces of Literature, or as you will learn when you take that course, many great stories have this structure in which a subplot helps us to better understand the main plot. Shakespeare is particularly adept at this approach. The dysfunctional family of King Lear and his daughters is mirrored by the problems that Gloucester is having with his boys; Hamlet's problematic relationships with his dead father, the ghost, and his new uncle-father is compared with young Fortinbras's relationship to his dead father, and Laertes's relationship to Polonius. Subplots deepen and extend the message of the main plot, so understanding Zechariah and his family should help us better understand the main Christmas narrative.

Consider, first, Zechariah. He was a priest in the division of Abijah. There were twenty-four priestly divisions, and they typically performed their service twice a year in the temple. Luke tells us that he is "upright in the sight of God" and "blameless" in following his commandments. He and Elizabeth are older, and they have no children; in first-century Jewish culture, barrenness was considered a great shame, even a judgment from God, particularly for the woman. On this particular day, Zechariah is selected by lot to burn the incense in the temple. A priest would only be selected once in a lifetime, if at all, for this special service.

As he is alone in the temple, Gabriel, which also could be translated "God's man," appears to Zechariah and gives him great news. He and Elizabeth are going to have a child. The shame of barrenness was to be removed, the whispering gossip of the neighbors was to be stopped, and the gift of a child was to be theirs. There should be great joy at hearing how God was to work in their lives. However, Zechariah responds to Gabriel, not with joy, but with disbelief.

"How can I be sure of this?" Zechariah says, which could also be translated "give me a sign," or even more harshly, "prove it to me." He is incredulous because, as he says, "I am an old man and my wife is well along in years." Here we have a righteous, God-fearing priest, who has served God his entire life. Zechariah is serving him in a very special way on this day in the temple, probably the most important day in his life as a priest. He is visited by an angel, God's man, and hears the promise that he has longed for most of his life, yet he cannot believe. Gabriel answers Zechariah's request and gives him a sign. He shuts Zechariah's mouth and perhaps even his ears (his friends have to use sign language to communicate to him later) until the time of the birth of his son. Gabriel also proclaims his authority. "I am Gabriel. I stand in the presence of God" (Luke 1:19).

In contrast, consider Mary. Gabriel comes to announce the birth of her child in a very similar way to that which he had done with Zechariah. The announcement is so similar that the Gospel seems to be inviting us to compare Mary's response with Zechariah's. Mary is young, probably fourteen to sixteen, a virgin at home, doing her normal work in her nondescript town of Nazareth. Zechariah is older, probably over forty, an established priest on the most important day in his career and at the center of the Jewish religious world, in the temple in Jerusalem. Gabriel comes to both of them to announce a miracle birth, a child to a long barren couple and a child to a virgin; of course, of the two miracles, Mary's is by far the greater. This news should be great joy to Zechariah, and perhaps great dread for Mary since she is unwed. Zechariah responds by saying "prove it to me." Mary responds first by wondering how this can happen biologically: "How will this be since I am a virgin?" But she soon readily accepts her role: "I am the Lord's servant," Mary answered. "May it be to me as you have said."

What should we make of this comparison? It is an example of how God tends not to follow our human expectations. Zechariah, the righteous religious leader whom we might pick to be at the center of God's drama on earth, actually stumbles a bit when offered a leading role. Mary, the seemingly bit player in the obscure town, willingly accepts her role at the center of God's redeeming plan for the world. Perhaps like you, I think that I am much closer to Zechariah than to Mary, much more caught up in my own righteousness and position than in listening for, and obeying, what God has for me to do, and much more ready to ask God to prove it than to accept what seems irrational. Perhaps as we imagine ourselves coming closer and closer to the center of God's drama, as we become the resident assistant, the ministry leader, the Students in Free Enterprise president, the pastor, the business leader, the professor, or the president of JBU, it becomes harder and harder for us to hear and believe the director of this drama.

So, how might we respond to this problem? How might we remain open to hearing God's direction? How might we resist our natural tendency to see ourselves as the center of God's world? Let us consider Zechariah's son, John, as a possible model. Gabriel made it very clear to Zechariah what John's role was to be: he was "to make ready a people prepared for the Lord." Zechariah confirms that calling when he regains his voice and sings a song of blessing over his newborn son: "And you, my child, will be called a prophet of the Most High; for you will go on before the Lord to prepare the way for him" (Luke 1:76). Gabriel and Zechariah both clearly defined John's role as that of the supporting character in the subplot: he was to prepare the way for the one who came after him; he was to prepare people to hear the way of Christ. And, John explicitly accepted his role in the subplot. When people began to ask him if he was the Christ, when he had the opportunity to move to the center of the stage, he quickly pointed people away from himself and toward Christ, toward the one who is "more powerful," "the thongs of whose sandals I am not worthy to stoop down and untie" (Mark 1:7).

Carey helps me to understand this point on a regular basis. She likes to leave me notes. Sometimes it is a sticky note on my computer screen, or in a book that I am reading, or in an email, or on my pillow. She has two favorite messages for me: the first one is "I love you" and the second one is "It is not about you." It is this second message that is the most helpful in this context. She sends that message to me when things are going really well. After we get news of a big donation to the university, I will find a sticky note on my computer screen saying "It is not about you," reminding me that God provides the blessing. She also sends them when things are going really poorly. When I am struggling with a problem in the budget, with a person, or with press, she will leave a note on my desk at home, "It is not about you," reminding me that God is also in control of the problems. In both cases, Carey's note that "it is not about you" reminds me that we are supporting characters, not the leads, in God's drama. I like the "I love you" notes better, but I need the "it is not about you" notes more, and I think that the truth of the first note leads her to send me the second.

And, despite what happens in our Christmas dramas at church, the Advent season really should remind us that "it is not about us," that we are the subplot, and remind us to fulfill our role as John the Baptist does, "making ready a people prepared for the Lord." Advent is not as much about the birth of Christ as it is about waiting for his coming again. It is not about remembering the past, but preparing the way for the future, and not about satisfaction with what is, but expectancy about what will be. It is not about the baby born in the manger, but about the King and Lord who is coming to rule.

So then what should we do? How should we fulfill our roles in the subplot? Consider again Isaiah's prophecy, repeated in the book of Luke: "Prepare the way for the Lord, make straight paths for him. Every valley shall be filled in, every mountain and hill made low. The crooked roads shall become straight, and the rough ways smooth. And all mankind will see God's salvation" (3:4-6). The metaphor is one of road building, and we are the construction crew. You know the road crew; they are the people who wear orange vests—kind of like the color of this "Acting on AIDS" shirt that I am wearing along with many of you today. We are called to prepare the way for Christ by fixing what is broken in our world so that people can see God's salvation. We make straight paths for him when we use only what we need in food or gas or electricity. We fill in the valley when we befriend the lonely person on our floor. We make the mountain and hill low when we visit the kids in Watts, Oklahoma and offer them hope that they are loved, not just by us, but by the Creator of the universe. We set straight the crooked roads when we humbly confront a friend who is cheating on his exam, or who is sleeping with his girlfriend, or who is making a racist joke. We make the rough ways smooth when we sit with the dying, or when we feed the hungry, or when we care for the orphan.

This Advent season, remember that we are called to "prepare the way" for Christ's coming again. "Prepare the way" by asking for forgiveness from your brother when you go home for Christmas, or "prepare the way" by volunteering to baby-sit for a young couple in your home church. As you leave to go home this semester, consider one specific action that you can take to "prepare the way" for Christ this Advent season—one specific pothole that you can fill in our broken world so that others can more easily see and hear of God's salvation. And, JBU, while we are called to prepare the way for Christ's coming again, we must always remind each other that we are not the way itself; we are the subplot, not the main drama. It is not about us, it is about him.

May it always be true of us.

CHAPTER 4

Second Semester

What Am I to Do? Vocation

Surveys of prospective students and parents always rate "career preparation" at, or near, the top of the list of reasons for selecting a college, and the pressure for students to discover what they will do for a job clearly remains high throughout their university experience. However, in our rapidly changing world, in which students will likely go on to have ten to twelve different jobs and work in three to four different professions, the focus on career preparation for the first job after college seems somewhat excessive. The capacities to think, write, speak, work with people, solve problems, learn new material, and to imagine innovative responses will likely be as important as any specific body of knowledge, and those capacities can be developed in almost any discipline. Moreover, education, in general, and Christ-centered education, in particular, should not just prepare students for careers. An educated follower of Jesus Christ should be better prepared to be a spouse and a parent, a citizen and a volunteer, a church leader and a community organizer. Followers of Christ should be educated to work as accountants or nurses, but also to discern the beauty of a concerto and to confront the injustice of racism. When God makes his call on our lives, he makes his call on our whole lives, and a Christ-centered university should seek to prepare students to respond to that all-encompassing sense of vocation.

Vocation in this broader sense is a frequent topic for me in chapel, particularly in the second semester when I am trying to turn students' attention outward, beyond the walls of the university. The first talk in this section happened during Family Weekend. Most universities designate at least one weekend a year for families to come and visit their sons or daughters on campus. The weekend allows both parents and siblings to have a view into the lives of their children at the university. Along with basketball games, a student talent show, class visits, and a reception at the president's house, we offer a special chapel on the Friday of that weekend to give as full a look into the life of the university as possible. I thought that it was important to present a broader understanding of vocation during Family Weekend so that parents would have some context for the discussions happening with their students at the university. I also borrowed an idea from a church in Dallas, and set up a "reverse" offering so as to make it very tangible for students and parents to think about the breadth of God's call on our lives. In this "reverse" offering, I had ushers hand out money to the audience and challenged them to spend it to further God's kingdom and then send me a note to tell me how they spent the money. As you might expect, this chapel caused a bit of a stir on campus; it is not often that a university president hands out money instead of asking for it. I received many notes for the next two months from students, parents, faculty, and staff. The JBU community was also interested in hearing how people used that money, so I gave a report about those notes later in the semester. I have included that report as the second reflection in this section.

In the third chapel address, I developed the theme of vocation by looking at the parable of talents and challenging students to see how they might use their money, gifts, time, and relationships to work for God as a form of worship. In the next reflection, I set this broader discussion of vocation in an eschatological context, trying to show students how what we do now for the kingdom of God is preparing us for what we will do for God in the new heaven and the new earth. In the final address of this section, I turn to the story of Daniel to suggest how it is only through the ordinary obedience in the everyday life that we are prepared to be ready for the challenge of extraordinary service to God.

God makes his call on our whole life, over all of our life. He gives us gifts to fulfill that calling, and exercising those gifts in his service should bring great joy. As Frederick Buechner says, "neither the hair shirt nor the soft berth will do. The place God calls you to is the place where your deep gladness and the world's deep hunger meet."[1]

Reverse Offering:
Spending for the Kingdom of God

Text: Luke 5:1-11

One day as Jesus was standing by the Lake of Gennesarret, with the people crowding around him and listening to the word of God, he saw at the water's edge two boats, left there by the fisherman, who were washing their nets. He got into one of the boats, the one belonging to Simon, and asked him to put out a little from shore. Then he sat down and taught the people from the boat.

When he finished speaking, he said to Simon, "Put out into the deep water, and let down the nets for a catch."

Simon answered, "Master, we've worked hard all night and haven't caught anything. But because you say so, I will let down the nets."

When they had done so, they caught such a large number of fish that their nets began to break. So they signaled their partners in the other boat to come and help them, and they came and filled both boats so full that they began to sink.

When Simon Peter saw this, he fell at Jesus' knees and said. "Go away from me, Lord; I am a sinful man." For he and all his companions were astonished at the catch of fish they had taken, and so were James and John, the sons of Zebedee, Simon's partners.

Then Jesus said to Simon, "Don't be afraid; from now on you will catch men." So they pulled their boats up on shore, left everything and followed him.

Our chapel theme for this semester has been "Citizens of the Kingdom," which I suggest is another way of saying that we should become "followers of Jesus Christ." That is ultimately our vocation, what

God has called you to do in this world. I want to look at Christ's call of his first disciples, his first followers, the first citizens of the kingdom of God, to see what Scripture has to teach us about being called to follow Christ.

The story of the call of Peter is likely a familiar one to many of you. Many of you have probably sung that Sunday school favorite: "I will make you fishers of men, fishers of men, fishers of men; I will make you fishers of men if you follow me." You are also likely quite familiar with the central features of the story. It is a great, if perhaps too often repeated Bible story, but we should not let the familiarity of this story deaden our perception to the radical call Jesus makes on us to become his followers.

This story is recounted in each of the synoptic gospels, Matthew, Mark, and Luke, but the Luke account is the most extensive and the most focused on Simon Peter. It is likely that this event is not Simon Peter's first meeting with Christ. The Gospel of John describes Simon Peter as having been first a disciple of John the Baptist and as having met Christ through John the Baptist. Christ is just beginning his public ministry and his message is clear: he is bringing in the kingdom of God. As Mark records it, Christ is saying over and over, "The time has come. . . . The kingdom of God is near. Repent and believe the good news" (1:15). Christ is gathering larger and larger crowds with this message and with his miracles, and he faces an increasingly growing practical problem. How will he speak to a large crowd so that all can hear him? He comes along the shore of the Sea of Galilee, sees an acquaintance, Simon Peter, and asks him for the use of his boat so that he can move offshore and use the natural amphitheater of the coast line to preach his message.

We need to understand a little about first-century fishing to understand this story fully. We are talking about commercial fishing, not recreational fishing, fishing with nets to bring in large amounts of fish to sell in the markets, not fishing with hooks or flies to catch and release. Indeed, this commercial fishing is very hard work. You notice that when Jesus comes upon Peter, he is cleaning his nets after a full night of fishing.

Typically, the fisherman in the Sea of Galilee would begin working at dusk and work through the night because the fish would come closer to the surface and to the shoreline as the water cooled in the evening. Moreover, while there were a variety of techniques for "net" fishing, it is probable that Peter and his friends had been using a "trammel net." A trammel net consists of three layers: the two outer layers were more loosely woven and the inner, middle layer was more finely meshed. The bottom of the net was weighted with lead to sink it to the bottom and the top of the net had cork to float. These nets came in sections about six feet in height and one hundred feet in length. Often the fishermen would connect five or six of these sections to form five hundred to six hundred feet of netting. You can just imagine the weight of that net even before it was filled with enmeshed fish.

The fishermen would take the net out into the deeper water and lower it into place. Then another group of fisherman would get along the shore or in the shallow end and make a lot of noise to drive the fish near the shore and into the net. The fish would go through the large netting on the outer layer, get enmeshed in the netting of the middle layer, but still push through the larger netting on the other outer layer, and then get fully entangled as they thrashed in the outer wall. The fisherman would then harvest the good fish by picking them out of the net, and then move along the shore to the next five-hundred-foot spot. They would typically be able to drop their nets ten to fifteen times in a night. When they finished, they returned to the shore to clean and untangle the nets and then sleep through the day. It was tedious and hard work. With that background, let's return to Scripture and see what Christ says about becoming his disciples, about being citizens of his kingdom.

"But because you say so"

Peter obeys Christ even though his instructions do not make sense and are not in his self-interest. Consider Peter's situation when Christ comes along.

He has been fishing all night with no results. He is in the midst of cleaning his nets to prepare for going out again the next night. Christ interrupts his cleaning of the nets and asks him to put the boat out so that he can speak. While it was inconvenient for Peter to put the boat out and he is tired, it is not a lot of work to row a few yards off shore. However, when Christ asks him to put the nets out into the water again, it is a different story. Peter objects, and you might think rightly so. Peter is the expert in fishing. He knows that it is better to fish at night rather than in the day because the fish are likely to be closer to the surface and the shore. He knows that he had no success last night. He knows that he and his men are tired from dropping that net ten to fifteen times. He also knows that if he puts out the nets, he will have to start all over again with the cleaning process to get the nets ready for the next night of fishing. Even so, Peter obeys Christ.

A follower of Jesus Christ should be characterized by obedience even when it might not seem to make sense. A citizen of the kingdom is honest in his work even when cheating would help them "get ahead" with a better grade. A follower of Christ volunteers in the community even if there is no networking possibility. Followers befriend the lonely and unlovable even if they are mocked by others. They do a job well even if no one will notice it. Christ calls his disciples to obey even if it does not make sense so that he can bring about the kingdom in his way. He is not looking for our professional expertise; he wants our obedience.

"Put out into the deep water."

I love Christ's injunction to go out to the "deep water." If you would permit me a bit of poetic license, let me explore the metaphor of Christ calling us to "go deep" as his disciples. He calls us to go into the deep water in our relationships with others. We should not be satisfied with superficial conversation, but instead address real issues in a person's life. It may mean that we need to confront a friend in love when they are off the track even if we may risk offending them, or it may be encouraging the shy student to come see you during office hours even when you would rather go home. Christ also calls us to go deep in our studies, not to be satisfied with doing enough to get by but to extend ourselves to learn beyond the requirements, and spending less time asking, "Will this material be on the test?" and more time asking, "How does fully understanding this material change the way that I think about this part of God's world?" Christ calls us to "go deep" with our time, perhaps spending less time in front of the television or the video game and more time in the neighborhood or working on homework. The reason that we should go for deep water is because that is where the fish are; it is where the real work of the kingdom occurs.

"So they signaled their partners."

Peter and Andrew could not bring in the fish by themselves. They had to call James and John to come help. Kingdom work is not typically done alone. We should be willing to work together, ask for help, and to share the load and the results with those around us.

"I am a sinful man."

Notice that Peter responds to Christ's call by becoming very sensitive to his own sinfulness. Christ's call to be a citizen of his kingdom begins with repentance. "The kingdom of God is near. Repent" (Matt. 1:15). There is a necessary link between being a follower of Jesus Christ and repenting of our sin. What does Peter have to repent for in this situation? Perhaps Peter is repenting for his own sense of pride. As the professional fisherman, Peter knows that Christ's request makes absolutely no sense. Peter doubts Christ and trusts his own expertise. Our sinfulness is often grounded in our pride. We want to do what we want to do when we want to do it. If Christ asks us to obey and it is inconvenient, we ignore the request. Being a citizen of the kingdom begins in recognizing our own sinfulness and repenting of it.

"Don't be afraid; from now on you will catch men."

Interestingly, Christ responds to Peter's confession by telling him "not to be afraid." There is a way in which becoming a citizen of the kingdom is a scary proposition. If we cannot always trust our own expertise, trust our own ways of handling things, trust that we are right in our way of seeing things, then we truly are "out of control" of the situation. If we should obey even if it does not make sense, then it can be a scary proposition. It is frightening to be out of control because we are giving away what we see as our power. Of course, this is exactly what God is asking us to recognize: that it is his kingdom, not ours; that he is in control, not us. However, the reward for turning over our control is that Christ allows us to work in a kingdom that has eternal stakes because it involves human beings. Christ reorients our perspective so that we are called to catch friends in his nets, to enmesh neighbors in his truth, to serve strangers in his fishing business, and to relish all the work because it has eternal value.

"They . . . left everything and followed him."

Notice Peter and his partners "left . . . everything and followed him." We should pause a moment to think about what they left. They left their commercial fishing business, which may have continued on because they had hired men, but which they were no longer going to control because they were not going to be involved every day in the business. They left their social network of friends, both the people that they worked with and the people in their synagogues and community. Most poignantly, they left their families, at least for stretches of time, to follow Christ. They didn't abandon their families—we know, for instance, that Christ visits Peter in his home and heals his mother-in-law, but the disciples certainly were absent from their families to follow Christ and do his work.

This last part is hard to accept sometimes. It is hard to accept that God's call for you to be his disciple may mean that you have to be apart from the ones that you love the most. I remember when I received a call from the search committee at John Brown University to serve as president. The first thing that I thought about was my oldest son, Chad, who was going into his senior year of high school. Carey and I had talked with him before we came down for the interview, and I knew that he would want to stay in Grand Rapids at least for the fall semester to play soccer and graduate with his class. I was not sure if I was ready to turn him loose; I was not sure if I was finished in parenting him; I was not sure if I was prepared to miss his soccer games or his band concerts. To be honest, I was not sure if I was sacrificing my son to take this job. As I was talking with a wise friend about the decision, he said to me: "Do you know that God cares more about Chad than you do? He is God's child before he is yours." His simple statement struck me to the core. I was worried about losing control of my son when I never had it in the first place. When Christ calls us to be citizens in his kingdom, it is okay for us to leave everything behind because Christ will take care of everything— our careers, our family, our reputations. He will likely not do it exactly as we planned, but he will take care of things in keeping with his plan.

For six weeks in chapel this semester, we have talked about becoming "followers of Jesus Christ, citizens of God's kingdom." I think that it is time that we start doing something about it. I have asked some students to hand out envelopes to everyone in the cathedral—students, parents, even siblings. Please take one envelope (and only one) and wait to open it.

When Christ called Peter and the others to follow him, he was also committing to invest his time, energy, and talents to teach and develop them into citizens of his kingdom. He was investing his life, quite literally his whole life, in the lives of his disciples. Similarly, when we invite you students to become a part of the JBU community, the faculty and staff are committing to invest their time, energy, and talents, their lives, in teaching and developing you so that you can become more fully citizens of the kingdom. Moreover, most of you have parents and/ or other family members who have also invested their lives and a good part of their resources to raise you as followers of Jesus Christ. You have youth leaders, summer camp counselors, church members, coaches, teachers, friends, and others, all of whom have spent lavishly of themselves so that you can be prepared to serve Christ and his kingdom.

So what are you doing with that investment in your life? How are you bringing about the kingdom of God? Now I want you to open the envelope. There is money inside. It is a "reverse" offering; instead of you giving to us, we are giving money to you. For most of you it is not a lot of money: most of you will receive $1 or $2, but twenty of you will receive $20, two of you will receive $50, and one of you will receive $100. Now, that is a rough approximation of the wealth in the United States. If we thought about it in a world context, the United States would likely be represented by the twenty-three people who received $20 or more out of the eight hundred people here today. God gives us different gifts. We are supposed to be responsible for the gifts that he gives us, and we in the United States have been given much.

I want the money to serve as a symbol of what others—your family, friends, teachers, coaches, and church members—have invested in you so that you can bring about the kingdom of God. And, here is my challenge to you. I want you to use that money in a way that brings about God's kingdom on earth. How so, you may ask? How can I do anything with so little money? It is not enough to make a difference.

Let me give you some possible examples. The kingdom of God is concerned for the poor, so a dorm floor could pool their money together and buy a goat for a family through Samaritan's Purse. It will cost you $21. The kingdom of God is concerned with the persecuted, so you could purchase three stamps and write letters to your senators and congressperson to defend those persecuted for their faith in China or the Middle East. The kingdom of God is concerned with those who mourn, so you could purchase a phone card and call a person who has lost a loved one. The kingdom of God is concerned with those in prison, so a dorm floor could get together and send a gift of encouragement to a prisoner through Prison Fellowship. The kingdom of God is concerned for those who are lost, so you can use your money to purchase an ice cream for a friend and share the gospel.

The kingdom of God is also concerned about righteous living, so some of you should take that dollar or two dollars and purchase coffee for a friend and talk to them about their struggles with promiscuity, or addiction to alcohol, or drugs, or greed. Others of you should buy a Coke and talk to the chaplain, a counselor, or your parents to confess to them your own struggles in these areas and your need for forgiveness. The whole JBU community—which means students, parents, faculty, staff, and administrators—should take seriously our obligation to call one another to be citizens of the kingdom in righteous living. And, of course, the great hope of our faith is that repentance leads to forgiveness. Christ called Peter to be a disciple as he fished along the Sea of Galilee, but that same Peter later denied Christ three times and returned to his fishing. Christ had to come to him again along the shores of Galilee and call him to repent and be restored. As the Gospel of Mark says, "The time has come. The kingdom of God is near. Repent and believe the good news!" (1:15). If you spend your money to bring about repentance and confession, it will be well spent.

I am taking a risk because I know that some of you will take the money and just spend it with little thought or care. It is the risk that each one of us takes everyday as we seek to become followers of Jesus Christ because to be a follower of Jesus Christ means that we invest completely in the lives of others without controlling whether the investment will pay off. God controls the results. It is Christ who saves and sanctifies and restores people, not us, but we are responsible to be a witness to others of that salvation, sanctification, and restoration. If we teach you nothing else at JBU, we should teach you to spend your life for others to bring about the kingdom of God. You could not make a better investment.

I would ask one more thing from you. If you spend the money to do a small thing to bring about God's kingdom, I would appreciate hearing about it. I want you to send me a brief note by campus mail or by email. I do not need to know names, but I want that note to serve as point of accountability for those who want to do the right thing but need a reminder to hold them responsible. It will also encourage me deeply to hear about how many of you are seeking to be followers of Jesus Christ because I know that a vast majority of you are. I look forward to receiving your notes as I look forward to watching your lives—to see how God's call on your life to be a follower of Jesus Christ will bring about his kingdom.

May it always be true of us.

A Theology of Gummy Worms:
A Report on Spending for the Kingdom of God

Text: 2 Thessalonians 2:16-17

*May our Lord Jesus Christ himself and God our Father, who loved us and
by his grace gave us eternal encouragement and good hope, encourage
your hearts and strengthen you in every good deed and word.*

Let me begin with a story. My son, James, is eight, and he is fascinated
with how close my office is to the Walker Student Center. We have just
given him the freedom to ride his bike over to campus with a friend,
and he has discovered that they sell candy and smoothies in the Walker
Student Center. So, every time he has a friend over to play at the house,
he wants to go on a bike ride so that he can get some candy and/or a
smoothie, typically about fifteen minutes before dinner. The other day,
when he figured out that my office was right next to the Walker Student
Center, he thought it was very cool because he thought that I must
be getting a candy and a smoothie every day. In his mind, the Walker
Student Center was a great place for stress release. He said to me, "You
know, Dad, when you have a long meeting or someone is cranky, you
can just walk over and get some gummy worms."

Even though James didn't realize it, I do think that he was expressing
a theological truth. We could call it the "theology of gummy worms," or
better yet, a theology of encouragement. Encouragement is a form of
love. Encouraging words offer comfort in times of stress, consolation
in times of grief, hope in a time of despair. And James got something
else right in our conversation: occasionally people do get cranky in the
president's office; occasionally, I do have to sit in long meetings with no
resolution to a difficult question in sight; occasionally, I do have a vice

president who calls to tell me a student is hurt, or an apartment is on fire, a faculty member has cancer, or a staff person is leaving; occasionally, I do receive a call from a board member, or a parent, or a community member with a complaint about how the university is operating. In other words, occasionally, I need a gummy worm or two to put things into perspective.

I have to thank you because the notes that you sent me over the last couple of months have been my "gummy worms" this past semester. I pull out the folder every couple of weeks and read again the creative ways that you used the money we disbursed in chapel to bring about the kingdom of God. It has been a deep source of encouragement to me, and I wanted to share them with you so that they may be an encouragement to you. I won't read all of them—we don't have time—but let me read a sample of them. I will try not to reveal names or identifying details, but I want to give you a sense of what people have done with God's money for his kingdom. Here are a few of them:

> Just wanted to let you know where the dollar went. I set out to spend the dollar toward purchasing diapers for a baby born to a fifteen-year-old mother. The excursion turned into a buying spree when another friend heard about my purchase and decided to buy many other things that the baby might need. The challenge to use the dollar turned into a challenge to use our monetary blessings.

> I wanted to thank you for the powerful challenge that you gave to JBU at Family Weekend chapel. I was one of the few who was given the responsibility of handling $20. As a college student, that's a lot of money. God immediately started bringing to mind a friend that I met for the first time this year. I asked her to go to dinner with me and we ended up talking for several hours. From what she said I don't believe she is a Christian but she is

here to learn what it's all about. She said most of what she sees around campus seems put-on. She wants people to be real with her. We learned a lot from each other that night and when I said I'd be paying for the meal with the money you gave me, she almost cried. She couldn't understand why I would spend the money on her. I said she was the only one I could think of (wanted to) spend the money on. I have continued to send her notes and look forward to our times together. Perhaps in a small way, I can be real with her and show her Christ for who He is. Thank you for helping make that possible and challenging me to look beyond myself.

Dr. Pollard, I was given $1 to put toward God's kingdom. With the dollar, I purchased some stamps. I picked up a few newspapers and cut out the comics from them. I then sat down and wrote notes to my friends that are overseas fighting in our military and sent the comics with notes of encouragement. Thank you for your speech during parent's chapel.

I donated my share of the money from chapel ($2) to the Northwest Arkansas Children's Shelter to buy new socks and hairbrushes for the girls who come there. I believe this was furthering God's kingdom because while it is a non Christian organization, it does minister to children who have been abused by providing them with love and safety and structure as well as meeting their physical needs.

Dr. Pollard, it's been a couple of weeks and I wanted to let you know what I've done with the money you handed out in chapel. That same week you spoke I learned that a childhood friend of mine is pregnant. She is not married and has drifted from her faith the last few years since she lost the support of her church family. I've watched her struggle since her father died of cancer in 2002 but I've never known how to reach out to her. The last time I saw her was Christmas of 2003, my sophomore year. As I've become more focused on my life at JBU I've distanced myself from my hometown and the people I grew up with, but I regret abandoning my friendship with this young woman that had always been so important in my life. So she was on my mind and in my heart when you challenged us in chapel, and I decided that I would use the dollar you gave me to reach out to her. I made her a baby blanket with the help of that dollar and I'm going home to Kansas this weekend to hand-deliver it to her, along with a letter apologizing for my distance in our friendship. I also want to extend the love of Christ to her reminding her of His unconditional love for her, her baby, and the baby's father. Thank you for your challenge, Dr. Pollard. I pray that it continues to abound in grace and love on this campus and beyond.

I just wanted to tell you that I used the $2 that I received in chapel to buy a coffee for one of the construction workers in my neighborhood. He really enjoyed it. I also asked him if he went to church. He said that he grew up a Seventh-Day Adventist but with his job he has not been to church in a long time. The conversation ended there because he had to get back to his job. The very odd thing is that I have not seen him since.

Hi, President Pollard. Sorry it's taken me so long to tell you what I did with the money from chapel during Family Weekend. My little brother (he's five and really sweet) and I decided to give it to my dad who is starting a ministry for families and children. It will support orphanages in Central and South America. Hopefully it will start a children's home with an evaluation center in Oklahoma. The center will also have facilities for young mothers that have nowhere else to go. It is also geared toward recruiting Christian foster families in Oklahoma. My dad is very passionate about it and he was very appreciative of the gift although it was small because Nathaniel is the one that handed it to him. Thank you so much for speaking at chapel. It impacted me and I really appreciate your heart for JBU and its students. Keep up the good work.

I just wanted to let you know that I am keeping the dollar you gave me in my wallet. I have attached Luke 12:48 to it so that every time I open my wallet I am reminded that to whom much is given much is required. It has reminded me that I need to take one of my friends out to dinner and tell him that I love him and that I am sorry that I have not been a better example of Christ to him over the past few years. A couple of my friends found out I was going to do this and they told me they wanted to give me their dollars to take him out to dinner. Just thought you should know. I would like for my dollar to reap 100 fold.

Dr. Pollard, thanks for the challenge to start living as a follower of Christ. I need to challenge myself more. I used my one dollar bill to help the Leadership class in their fundraiser. Each group in the Leadership class completes an original service project. One particular group decided to have a car wash to raise money for the Genesis House, the local homeless shelter. I donated my money to the group of students to add to their total amount of money they raised. The total amount of money will go directly to the Genesis House to provide food and other physical needs to homeless people in the community. I plan to spend some time helping out at the Genesis House in the future so I can serve the community more. I look forward to any opportunities this will provide. I wanted to make sure you knew how I made use of my money. Thanks again!

Dear President. I truly enjoyed and was encouraged by your speech in chapel. I spent my dollar on peanut butter for kids at the local food kitchen.

Hey, Dr. Pollard. I received $20 in chapel last Friday. You mentioned the Heifer project. I always thought that it would be cool to buy an animal from them so I used the money to buy a flock of geese. Not only do geese lay eggs, but their feathers are great for stuffing pillows! Plus, they make excellent watchdogs.

Hey, Dr. Pollard, I just wanted to let you know that I gave the dollar I received in chapel to Clyde Villon. He is a six-year-old boy from the Philippines that I and a few other guys support through Compassion International, which has a ministry on campus. I think your illustration was a very good idea. Money is the one thing that everyone pays attention to. Hopefully I will keep the memory with me for a long time and be reminded every time I reach in my wallet that I am only a steward of the King.

Hello, good sir, my apologies for my tardiness. I struggled for quite some time with how to spend my dollar. I did not want to grasp for a pious cause to give to when I didn't already feel the conviction to be involved with the cause before your chat/sermon/lecture. For example, I decided after some prayer that giving to Genesis House would be an empty gesture on my part. It felt like throwing money at the problem. I was stuck. The dollar forced me to make a mental list of the priorities that I should have for the kingdom. If I only had a dollar, I thought the best impact for the dollar would be on some divine calling that I had already invested in. I took the dollar and bought my wife a flower.

Dr. Pollard, thank you for your pointed but sincere challenge to JBU. I've decided to use my dollar to contribute to "Buckets of Love" going to tsunami survivors. The buckets will contain items useful in dealing with the current environmental situation as well as fun gifts to lift the spirits of people receiving them. $1 will buy four bouncy balls. Can't you see the delight in four sets of eyes that have seen only desolation since December . . . they'll be seeing a ray of hope in this little package of love!

In 2 Thessalonians 2:16-17, Paul ends a section of instruction with this prayer: "May our Lord Jesus Christ himself and God our Father, who loved us and by his grace gave us eternal encouragement and good hope, encourage your hearts and strengthen you in every good deed and word."

Let me offer two quick points from this passage: first, it is Christ and God our Father who is both the source and the means of encouragement and hope; and second, the work of encouragement is important work. We are called to encourage people's hearts, to help lift their spirits, and to minister to their emotional lives because it will strengthen them to do good deeds and speak good words.

So thank you for the ways in which you have strengthened me this semester, and I would encourage you to continue to spend yourself in furtherance of God's kingdom.

May it always be true of us.

Work as Worship: The Parable of the Talents

Text: Matthew 25:14-30

Again, it will be like a man going on a journey, who called his servants and entrusted his property to them. To one he gave five talents of money, to another two talents, and to another one talent, each according to his ability. Then he went on his journey. The man who had received the five talents went at once and put his money to work and gained five more. So also, the one with the two talents gained two more. But the man who had received the one talent went off, dug a hole in the ground and hid his master's money.

After a long time the master of those servants returned and settled accounts with them. The man who had received the five talents brought the other five. "Master," he said, "you entrusted me with five talents. See, I have gained five more."

His master replied, "Well done, good and faithful servant! You have been faithful with a few things; I will put you in charge of many things. Come and share your master's happiness."

The man with the two talents also came. "Master," he said, "you entrusted me with two talents; see, I have gained two more."

His master replied, "Well done, good and faithful servant! You have been faithful with a few things; I will put you in charge of many things. Come and share your master's happiness!"

Then the man who had received the one talent came. "Master," he said, "I knew that you are a hard man, harvesting where you have not sown and gathering where you have not scattered seed. So I was afraid and went out and hid your talent in the ground. See, here, is what belongs to you."

His master replied. "You wicked, lazy servant! So you knew that I harvest where I have not sown and gather where I have not scattered seed?

Well then, you should have put my money on deposit with the bankers, so that when I returned I would have received it back with interest.

"Take the talent from him and give it to the one who has ten talents. For everyone who has will be given more, and he will have an abundance. Whoever does not have, even what he has will be taken from him. And throw the worthless servant outside, into the darkness, where there will be weeping and gnashing of teeth."

We need to see this parable in its context. It is toward the end of a rather long section in Matthew in which Christ is answering his disciples' questions about why he will go away, what they should do while he is away, and what to look for when he will return. In particular, this parable addresses what we should do until he comes again, what he expects from us in this life, what we are called to do, and what our vocations are in this world. I want to look at this parable in two different ways, first focusing on several phrases that characterize the relationship between the master and the three different servants, and then focusing on the talents.

The master "entrusted his property" to his servants.

The parable begins by telling us that the master "entrusted his property" to his servants, and there are two things to notice here. First, what may be obvious but still bears repeating: the master owns the property. He owns the property before, during, and after he has given it to the servants. We should acknowledge that this world belongs to God and that we are only stewards of it. Second, while the master is away, he entrusts the property to his servants. In other words, Christ is saying to his disciples and to us that he trusts us to use his things, his world, and do his work on earth while he is away. Now trust always involves risk because the person that you trust may not live up to your expectations. It is one of the amazing truths of our faith that God takes the risk to give his servants his world in order to do his work. It is a great responsibility but also a great task. The God of the universe has confidence in us to do his work in his world.

The master gave "each according to his ability."

Notice that in this account of the parable, unlike the account in Luke, the master gives different amounts to the servants based on their ability. Matthew makes an important point here. While we are equal in our sin and our need for salvation, God does make distinctions in the gifts that he gives his people. Some of us are given more intelligence, more financial resources, more emotional health, more educational opportunities, more physical beauty, or more enriching relationships than others. We notice these distinctions and they tend to bother us, sometimes to the point of becoming paralyzing preoccupations. Why am I not as smart as that guy in calculus? Why don't I have the job offers of that woman in graphic design? Why don't I have as many friends as my roommate? Why does God seem to give more to my friend than to me?

This game of comparison, this measuring of your gifts against another person's, this constant evaluating of whether you have gotten your fair share of God's resources, is a deadly exercise. It can consume you in jealousy and bitterness. It has for me in different times in my life. The master treats his servants fairly, but he does not treat them exactly the same, nor should we expect him to. It is his property, and he can distribute it as he sees fit. God calls each of us to be responsible for the gifts that he has given to us, not for the gifts that he has given to another.

"After a long time, the master of those servants returned and settled accounts with them."

The master comes back, and he expects a return on his money. Our God is a God of accountability, a God who settles accounts with his servants, a God who asks us what we have done with his gifts, a God who expects us to use his gifts to expand and enrich his kingdom. I must admit that it is a bit terrifying to think in these terms. The God of the universe has given us his world, including his people, and he will want a report on what we have done with it and with them. None of us looks forward to accountability, but most of us probably would admit that accountability does encourage us to use our gifts more fully. An exam helps us to study more thoroughly, a project deadline helps us to focus more intensely, an accountability relationship helps us to live more righteously, and a prayer companion helps us to pray more regularly.

God expects us to perform with the gifts that he has given us. While this expectation may cause anxiety, we should take comfort in knowing that God only expects us to use the gifts that he has given us, not some gifts that he has not given us. We should take comfort that God has confidence that we can use those gifts.

"Putting the money to work" or "digging a hole"

It is instructive to compare the first two servants with the third. All three servants probably recognize the character of the master. As the third servant says to him, you are a "hard man, harvesting where you have not sown and gathering where you have not scattered seed." Knowing this, the first two servants immediately take their money and put it to work, which is a risk. There is no assurance that they will be able to earn a return on the master's money. They may fail and have to come back with less than what they started. However, the first two servants overcome their fear of failure and take the risk in order to meet the expectation of the master. The third servant is so afraid that he buries his money in a field, a common practice in New Testament times to keep money safe. The fear of losing the money prevents him from using it.

We too fear failure. We fear trying to use our God-given gifts because we may fail. Indeed, it is a part of our culture of cool, a culture of always setting low expectations so that you can always meet them. My son, Chad, explained it to me this way. He said that in high school he consciously developed a reputation with his friends that he didn't work hard in his studies. He did this so that if he got a good grade, it was because he was naturally brilliant and so cool; if he got a bad grade, it was because he did not care that much and so he was still cool. It was more important to look cool than to achieve, more important not to fail in front of his friends than to use his gifts to the fullest. This is the mindset of the third servant. Notice too that the third servant really blames the master for his failure. It was because you are so hard that I could not take a risk with your property. He never accepts responsibility for using the gifts the master has given to him, which is why, in part, the master is so harsh in his judgment. Being ready for God's return is not simply playing it safe in life and doing no harm. He expects a return on the investment of the gifts that he has entrusted to us.

In short, this parable teaches that while we wait for God's return, we have work to do, that God entrusts us with his gifts to do his work, that we should not spend much time or energy comparing our gifts to others. We should expect to be held accountable for how we use his gifts. We should not be paralyzed by the fear of failure but rather take risks to use these gifts. And we should use them to multiply his kingdom.

Okay, but what resources does God give to us? How do we understand what the parable means, both literally and metaphorically, by the term talent?

We should recognize that "talent" in this passage literally means money. A talent was a measure of weight for precious metal that was somewhere between fifty to ninety pounds. And so, when the master hands out five, two, and one talents, he is entrusting the servants with a lot of wealth. Living here in the United States, we too have been given a great amount of wealth. Indeed, even as college students, you have access to wealth that far exceeds most of the rest of the world. How can we use the gift of what is God's money to bring about the kingdom of God? I am sorry if you came to chapel today because you heard that the president gives out envelopes of money on Family Weekend. I am not going to do that again this year. Instead, I have another example.

In mid-January, I received a note from a student, Nathan, inviting me to a tailgate party to raise funds for children in Uganda, children who are being kidnapped and forced to become child soldiers. I was out of town that night and couldn't make the party, but that didn't deter Nathan. A day or so later, I received another note saying that they had raised $740 at the tailgate party and inviting me to a charity-sponsored intramural game between El Bigote (the big mustaches) and ISSOD (Intramural Soccer Squad of Death). I had an interest in going to the game because I play soccer with ISSOD. I have the uniform to prove it. However, I learned that the game started at 10:00 P.M., which was well past my bedtime, so I again had to send my regrets. Nathan was again undeterred. He sent me another note saying that total contributions were up to $920. I asked him to come and tell me more. We talked and I found out that he was storing the money in a shoebox in his room. I offered him the safe in the business office and told him that Carey and I could also make a modest contribution. By the time he came by my office to pick up our check, Nathan and his friends had raised over $1,300 to bring about the kingdom of God in Uganda. That is a great example of JBU students multiplying the wealth and creativity that they have been given to bring about God's kingdom.

Of course, as even this example shows, God entrusts us with more than just wealth. He also gives us abilities and skills that we can use for his kingdom. Let me give you another example. Carey and I had the privilege of going to the music department's production of the *Pirates of Penzance* last week. The students in that production can act, and sing, and even dance. Indeed, the level of performance was already high, and then Allie broke into her first solo; wow—it was beautiful, and beauty is a part of God's kingdom. I also enjoy the beauty in watching our shooting guard, Brandon, run through fourteen picks to get open to launch one of those graceful three-point shots, or defensive stopper, Ashley, stepping into the lane to take yet another charge. Using one's mind to its fullest capacity is also a thing of beauty. Exercising any of these talents involves the risk of failure, sometimes very public failure, but these students have taken that risk and so contribute their skills to building God's kingdom.

Time is another one of the resources that God gives us, another one of our talents. Indeed, it is one of the most precious of the gifts that God gives us. I wonder, however, how well we use this gift. I just read a study that said that the average college student spends three and a half hours a day watching television. Is that the best use of your time? How much time do you spend playing video games? Or on Facebook, just scrolling through the Internet, or going to the mall? None of these activities are necessarily bad in moderation—recreation is a part of our calling—and sometimes they are useful in developing relationships. Indeed, I had a student write a paper once in which he argued that playing video games was vital for relationships among guys because it was easier to talk about serious matters while you were blowing somebody up together on the screen. We have television, and Xbox, and the Internet in our home; however, I do wonder sometimes about when God asks us to account for our time: will we really want to say that we were the *Halo* champion of our residence hall or that we watched every episode of *Lost*? We should all think about how we use God's gift of time to invest it in a way that will produce a return for his kingdom.

Finally, I believe that people are the most important gift that God gives to us and that we have a deep and abiding responsibility to develop the gifts of other people so that they will contribute to God's kingdom. It is what Kristen seeks to do through organizing a mentoring program for students through the local camp. It is what Valerie is seeking to do by meeting with Willie, a fourth-grade student, to help him with his homework or talk with him about the struggles and joys of growing up in a bilingual home. It is what your parents have done for you by sacrificing to enable you to attend JBU. It is what you do for your parents when you call them just to say that you love them. Each one of us has been given other people, and we are responsible to help them develop into men and women of God. When God asks for an account of how we have fulfilled our responsibility to develop other people—to develop our family, our friends, our neighbors, our colleagues, our employees, our students—what will we be able to say? God has entrusted other people to you; will you be able to show a return on that trust?

Let me close with a final illustration. This Christmas, when I received an iPod Nano as a present, I told my kids that I was now officially cool. It did, however, take me the better part of three weeks to figure out how to put music on it, so I was not quite as cool as I thought. One of the albums that I put on my Nano was by the cellist Yo-Yo Ma. I know, again, classical music on the Nano is probably not really cool. I have had this album for perhaps ten years, but I had never listened to it on headphones. As I was listening to the second piece, Bach's Cello Suite #3 in C, I heard for the first time, Yo-Yo Ma's breathing just under the music. He is breathing hard—almost panting. The piece is a challenging one, and he is really working at it, expending every ounce of his skill and effort to achieve this thing of beauty. And, I thought to myself, what a wonderful example of what we should do with our gifts from God. When we are writing a paper, we should be breathless as we wrestle words into meaning. When we are studying in the library, we should be panting to understand the concepts. When we are counseling a friend, we should be winded by our concern for their well-being. When we love a friend, or a child, or a parent, we should be breathing hard in our effort to affirm them as a child of God. We should live our lives fully extended in exercising our gifts from God. That is work as worship; that is a life of calling; and, that characterizes the life of a servant whose master will say to him or her at the end, "Well done, good and faithful servant! Come and share your master's happiness."

May it also be true of us.

Calling: Occupying Our Room in the Father's House

Text: John 14:1-6, 15-17

"Do not let your hearts be troubled. Trust in God; trust also in me. In my Father's house are many rooms; if it were not so, I would have told you. I am going there to prepare a place for you. And if I go and prepare a place for you, I will come back and take you to be with me that you also may be where I am. You know the way to the place where I am going."

Thomas said to him, "Lord, we don't know where you are going, so how can we know the way?"

Jesus answered, "I am the way and the truth and life. No one comes to the Father except through me. . . .

If you love me, you will obey what I command. And I will ask the Father, and he will give you another Counselor to be with you forever—the Spirit of truth. The world cannot accept him, because it neither sees him nor knows him. But you know him, for he lives with you and will be in you.

Today, I want to talk with you a bit about our Father's house, about the dwelling place of God. Now if you would ask young children, "Where does God dwell or live?" as I asked my son James, they will most often point to the sky and say "heaven." Indeed, many of us probably have concepts of heaven as the place that we go after death, concepts that have been shaped by our experiences of family devotions, Sunday school materials, Veggie Tales, or other popular culture representations. Those representations are often of St. Peter at the gates of heaven inviting or declining entrance into heaven for people who have just died; heaven is portrayed as having streets paved with gold and large mansions with people flying around with wings on their backs and harps in their hands.

Now these popular representations are not entirely fanciful. In this passage, Christ suggests that he is preparing a place for his disciples. Revelation does describe, at least metaphorically, the New Jerusalem as a place in which the streets are made of pure gold. Moreover, Scripture teaches that absence from the body is presence with the Lord. However, these popular representations have also distorted our understanding of heaven and earth, of where God dwells, and, perhaps, of the whole point of Christianity which is not simply that we go to heaven when we die, but that eventually heaven and earth will become one in God's new creation and that we will dwell with God there. We have a vocation now. We are called to live in the present as a people called to that future, to live in our sin-soaked world as a people that will eventually live in this new creation, to begin now to occupy our rooms in the Father's house, the dwelling place of God. Let me explain by examining this passage more closely.

The context for these verses is important. Christ is in the upper room with his disciples; he has just washed their feet, revealed to them that Judas was going to betray him, explained to them that he was going where they couldn't follow, and predicted that Peter would deny him three times before morning.

"Do not let your hearts be troubled. Trust in God; trust also in me."

So, we understand why Christ begins this passage with words of comfort: "Do not let your hearts be troubled. Trust in God; trust also in me." The disciples have much to be troubled about. Christ's actions and words were making very little sense, and what sense they were making was terrifying. He was not to be long with them and they could not follow him; moreover, two of his closest followers, their friends, were either going to betray or deny him. The disciples must have felt as if events were spinning out of control and that all of their expectations were being dashed.

Some of you come this morning with your hearts troubled. You are homesick and wondering if you made the right decision to come to

JBU. Others of you are worried that you will not be able to succeed in the classroom. Others have heavy hearts because of what is going on at home in your family. Some of you are troubled by the ever-increasing pace of the devastation of God's created world. Others of us have lost a loved one or have friends or family battling with serious illness. Others are troubled by trying to reconcile the poverty that you saw in Uganda or Guatemala with the richness of the resources here. Still others of us have hearts troubled by larger world events, by the wars in Iraq and Darfur, the earthquake in Peru, or the devastation of Hurricane Dean in Mexico. Others of you may recognize that this is your final year here at JBU and your hearts are troubled about your future. What am I going to do with my life after JBU? We live in a world broken by sin, so it is not surprising that many of us have troubled hearts.

But to all of us whose hearts are troubled this morning, Christ offers his words of comfort. "Do not let your hearts be troubled. Trust in God; trust also in me." Notice that comfort comes only when we trust in God's character as it is revealed in Christ's life. Our hope comes from God, not from our capacity to be clever or popular or persistent or optimistic or even faithful. Living in a world broken by sin, we should expect to be troubled, but Christ constantly reminds us that it is still his world despite the sin and trouble. As he says later to the disciples in John 16, "In this world you will have trouble. But take heart. I have overcome the world."

"In my Father's house are many rooms."

Christ then gives them reason for hope by saying, "In my Father's house are many rooms; if it were not so, I would have told you. I am going there to prepare a place for you. And if I go and prepare a place for you, I will come back and take you to be with me that you also may be where I am." I want to take a moment and reflect on Christ's use of the phrase "in my Father's house are many rooms." We should take comfort that there are many rooms in the Father's house, for I think that it suggests that

Christ desires all people to dwell with him and that he accepts all sorts of different people into his home: people as diverse as Nicodemus, the Samaritan woman at the well, Zacchaeus, and Paul. Christ is also preparing a unique room for each of us in his Father's house. Christ knows our talents, limitations, desires, and fears, and the room that he prepares for each of us will challenge, stretch, and encourage us to flourish as the distinct child of God that he has created each of us to be. Each of us has a different calling, a different thing that God wants us to do.

I admit that I understand this metaphor through my own experience as a father. When we were asked to come to JBU three years ago, one of the hardest parts about the transition was sitting down with our kids and telling them that they were going to have to move and leave their friends, their schools, and their home. Their hearts were troubled by the news. James was then almost eight and he cried because he would never get to play on the big playground at his new school. Emma was almost eleven and she cried about leaving Erica, Pauline, and other friends. Ben was almost fourteen and he was just angry. Chad was almost seventeen, and he made it clear that he wasn't coming, that he was going to stay in Grand Rapids. As I looked at my children, and saw that their hearts were deeply troubled by this decision, I searched for ways to bring comfort, one of which was to promise them that we would build a house and design rooms for each of them.

Now, that process worked relatively smoothly with the boys. Chad stayed in Grand Rapids to finish high school and start college, so he was not in need of a room in our new home. Ben and James were happy for their rooms to fit into the overall design of the house. As long as their beds were comfortable, their posters were on the walls, and there was food in the refrigerator, they didn't care much about the particulars. However, my Emma was different. Growing up in house full of brothers, her room was her haven in a mostly male-oriented world. She did not want earth tones like the rest of the house; instead, she chose bright egg-shell blue for her bedroom walls and shocking pink with black accents for her bathroom. When Matt Pearson, our architect and JBU professor, saw the colors, he kindly suggested that her room glowed and that we should consider a change. I tended to agree with him about the colors, but I knew that we should not change them. It was her room, not mine nor the architect's. I knew that she would flourish in this room with its special reading chair next to the window and a back porch in which she could lose herself in her imagination. As her father, I wanted to build a room that would enable her to flourish in the ways that God has made her. I expect that Christ has a similar desire for us, preparing us rooms not just to meet our needs, but to stretch us to become the people that he wants us to be.

Another thing to notice about this metaphor of rooms is that it conveys God's desire to dwell with us. It is a theme throughout Scripture. God is there walking in the Garden of Eden with Adam and Eve until their sin drives them out of their garden home. He promises Abraham, Isaac, and Jacob to abide with them in the Promised Land. God leads Moses and the people of Israel with a cloud during the day and the pillar of fire at night, and then promises them: "I will put my dwelling place among you, and I will not abhor you. I will walk among you and be your God, and you will be my people" (Lev. 26:11-12). God then dwells with his people through the Ark of the Covenant, an ark that leads them through the wilderness, across the river Jordan, and in conquering their enemies. God dwells with his people through the temple, the first one built by Solomon and then destroyed by Nebuchadnezzar, and the second one built by the exiles who returned to Jerusalem and then restored by Herod just before Christ's birth. As you trace this history, you recognize how often Scripture describes God dwelling with his people through a particular place—the garden, the Promised Land, the ark, and, most notably, the temple. Heaven and earth interlock and overlap as God dwells with his people through a particular place.

Now, as N. T. Wright suggests, tracing this history is important, for it gives context for the radical shift that Christ is suggesting in this passage, the radical shift from God dwelling with his people through a particular place to God dwelling with his people through the actions of a particular person—his son, Jesus Christ. To understand this transformation, we have to see how Christ challenges the Jewish understanding of the temple. Early in the Gospels, Christ calls the temple his "Father's house" when he visits it with his parents as a young boy and when he drives out the moneychangers. He then claims that the temple will be destroyed and rebuilt in three days, In other words, he suggests that he replaces the temple. He pours out his life on the cross to replace the blood sacrifices of the temple to make us right with God. Indeed, when Christ dies, the temple curtain is cut in two from top to bottom to suggest that Christ has literally made a new way for God to dwell among his people. The cross literally becomes not only the place, but also the event, through which Christ is suspended between heaven and earth, and the eternal and the temporal become one, heaven and earth interlock, and God's future kingdom is announced in the present.

"But you know him, for he lives with you and will be in you."

This transformation of the meaning of the temple is not quite complete. Not only does Christ, through his death and resurrection, replace the temple and thereby radically open up a new means for God to dwell with his people, but also, as the second part of our reading today suggests, Christ also asks his Father to "give you another Counselor to be with you forever—the Spirit of truth. . . . you know him, for he lives [dwells] with you and will be in you." In short, when Christ asks the Father to send the Holy Spirit to dwell within us, we become the temple of God, both as individuals ("Don't you know that you yourselves are God's temple and that God's Spirit lives [dwells] in you? . . . God's temple is sacred, and you are that temple" [1 Cor. 3:16-17]) and collectively as the church

("... Christ Jesus himself as the chief cornerstone. In him the whole building is joined together and rises to become a holy temple in the Lord. And in him you too are being built together to become a dwelling in which God lives by the spirit" [Eph. 2:20-22]). Our lives, both individually and collectively, can be the place where earth and heaven interlock and overlap, where the temporal and eternal meet, where we glimpse and work for God's future kingdom in the here and now, and where God dwells and makes himself known to his people.

"I am the way and the truth and life."

Consider again the phrase, "in my Father's house are many rooms." Let me suggest that we should begin to occupy those rooms in the Father's house even now; we become the place in which God dwells, not only in some distant future after we die, but also right now in this present life. He prepares us to be places in which God can dwell. How does he prepare us? He asks us to follow him. Good doubting Thomas asks the obvious question: "Lord, we don't know where you are going, so how can we know the way?" (John 14:5). And Christ tells him again of this radical new way to dwell with God: "I am the way and the truth and the life. No one comes to the Father except through me" (John 14:6). Christ is the way to God; Christ is the truth of God; Christ is the life of God. Christ offers a new way for God to dwell with his people. He offers us a new way to understand the true character of God, as a righteous, holy judge, but also as broken, redeeming savior. He offers us a new way to live life, as a conquering of death, but also as working for him to bring about his kingdom and new creation. Worship is no longer a journey to the temple, but following the way set out by the person of Jesus Christ.

As N. T. Wright suggests, Jesus' death and resurrection is not primarily about "going to heaven after you die"; instead Christ's death and resurrection hold out the promise that the whole world will be fixed. Not only will we have new bodies, but the whole creation will be made new and unblemished. While the complete fulfillment of this promise is in the future, Christ's death and resurrection also calls for us to work for it even now, to work toward the health, peace, love, justice, and wholeness that will characterize the new heaven and the new earth. We have good work to do even while we live in this temporal, broken, sinful world.

So what might that good work look like for us here at JBU? How might we begin to move into our rooms in the Father's house? How might we begin again to follow the way to God, the truth of God, and the life of God? How might we begin to hear God's call on our lives? Let me give you just a few illustrations, the categories of which come from Wright's book *Simply Christian*.

God's new creation will be a place in which justice reigns, so we should seek to bring about justice now. However, justice is not simply a question of us being on the right side and some other people being on the wrong. Justice draws its line through the hearts of each of us. Justice here at JBU involves simple things such as doing your academic work honestly, reconciling with those that you wrong, and fulfilling your promises. But it also should involve working for justice in complex matters: it may involve studying the reconciliation between Catholics and Protestants in Northern Ireland and applying lessons from there to other situations of strife; it may involve studying the best teaching methods and applying those methods to the kids at risk in Siloam Springs or Watts; it may involve changing our habits of consumption, reducing the waste in our daily life, so that we preserve God's resources for future generations. It may also involve creating new businesses in Guatemala City or in Bentonville so that people can be gainfully employed and provide for their families, or studying organic chemistry to prepare for the Medical College Admission Test (MCAT) while at the same time volunteering at St. Francis clinic or in Ethiopia to care for the sick and dying. The way of Christ is a way of justice, and we should follow that way even now.

Next, in God's new creation, people will have relationships that enable them to flourish. We are made to be in right relationship with others, so we should seek to bring about such relationships even now. Again, much of this work is unspectacular even if it is difficult to do: it is being kind and patient with your roommate, asking for forgiveness from your resident assistant, loving the unlovely by inviting the guy down the hall to play intramurals. It is dressing modestly; it is controlling our sexual desires; it is being willing to learn from a person who looks, thinks, and acts differently than you. And, it does not only happen here on campus: it is honoring your parents even if their marriage is breaking apart. It is serving the seniors in your church even if they do not like your electric guitar, and treating your boss with respect even if she does not appreciate you. The way of Christ is the way of right relationships with others and we should follow that way even now.

Third, God's new world will be a world of beauty, and we should recognize, create, and preserve beauty even now. Beauty is found all around us: in the butterflies that landed on this text as my wife was reading it, in the elegance of a bridge designed by our engineers, in the outside hitter stretching to the edge of the net to finish her kill, and in the soprano solo during Candlelight. There is beauty in the acing of an exam, in preserving the watershed around Sager Creek, in the clarity of the design of a Web page, and in the restoration of deteriorating buildings. Certainly our world is filled with ugliness, but when we recognize, create, and preserve beauty, we catch a glimpse of God's future world which will be filled to its edges with beauty.

God's new world will also be a world of worship, a world in which we proclaim God's glory in word, song, prayer, and life, and even now we can live out that world of worship. Someone just asked me what I most look forward to in the fall, and I told that person that it was the students returning to sing in chapel. You bring glory to God through your singing. You bring glory to God through reading his Word and listening in chapel. You bring glory to God through praying alone and in groups. You bring glory to God by worshiping in churches on Sunday. You bring glory to God in these traditional forms of worship, but I would encourage you to see all of your life as having the potential to be a sacrifice of praise to God. You worship him in the ways in which you seek justice, in establishing right relationship with others, in creating and sustaining beauty; indeed, in every aspect of your life you can point toward his future kingdom.

So, JBU, hear again the gospel of Jesus Christ. If you are a follower of Jesus, a follower of the way, the truth, and the life, then you are the temple of the Holy Spirit: you are occupying a room in the Father's house; you are the dwelling place of God; and he has called you to do his eternal work even now in this bent and troubled world. It is time for us to begin again this work, time to buckle up and be about our Father's business. It is time both to pray and live out the Lord's prayer: "Our Father, which art in heaven, Hallowed be thy name. Thy kingdom come. Thy will be done, as in heaven, so on earth" (Luke 11:2 KJV).

May it always be true of us.

Ordinary Obedience

Text: Daniel 6:10-12, 16-23

Now when Daniel learned that the decree had been published, he went home to his upstairs room where the windows opened toward Jerusalem. Three times a day he got down on his knees and prayed, giving thanks to his God, just as he had done before. Then these men went as a group and found Daniel praying and asking God for help. So they went to the king and spoke to him about his royal decree: "Did you not publish a decree that during the next thirty days anyone who prays to any god or man except you, O king, would be thrown into the lion's den?

The king answered, "The decree stands—in accordance with the laws of the Medes and Persians, which cannot be repealed."

So the king gave the order, and they brought Daniel and threw him into the lions' den. The king said to Daniel, "May your God, whom you serve continually, rescue you!

A stone was brought and placed over the mouth of the den, and the king sealed it with his own signet ring and with the rings of his nobles, so that Daniel's situation might not be changed. Then the king returned to his palace and spent the night without eating and without any entertainment being brought to him. And he could not sleep.

At the first light of dawn, the king got up and hurried to the lions' den. When he came near the den, he called to Daniel in an anguished voice. "Daniel, servant of the living God, has your God whom you serve continually, been able to rescue you from the lions?"

Daniel answered, "O king, live forever! My God sent his angel, and he shut the mouths of the lions. They have not hurt me, because I was found innocent in his sight. Nor have I ever done any wrong before you, O king.

The king was overjoyed and gave orders to lift Daniel out of the den. And when Daniel was lifted from the den, no wound was found on him, because he had trusted in his God.

Daniel and the lions' den, clearly one of the top ten Old Testament Bible stories: a story that you have likely heard many times in Sunday school and in church, and a story that you have likely seen enacted time and again by our friends from Veggie Tales. Of course, the problem with familiarity is that it breeds contempt or complaisance. We know the story so well that we don't actually read or hear the text. Perhaps today we can make this story "strange" again by understanding how Daniel learned to "serve continually his God."

Daniel's dance in the lions' den is one of the dramatic high points of his life. It is the defining conflict between being loyal to God or loyal to the world, the defining choice for martyrdom rather than compromise. Many of us are drawn to these dramatic moments of confrontation. We want the big vision: the vision of ending poverty with Bono, or curing AIDS with World Vision, or eliminating abortion in the United States, or of reversing global warming. Don't get me wrong, these big visions are clearly a part of seeking to bring about Christ's kingdom in a world broken by sin. It is difficult, however, to sustain a commitment to the big vision if it does not come out of a life of ordinary obedience. Are we called more to be obedient than spectacular, more to be faithful than dramatic, or more to be sacrificial than significant? Daniel, I would suggest, lived a life of ordinary obedience through which God prepared him for extraordinary service. Indeed, we need to understand the ordinary obedience of Daniel in chapter one before we can understand the extraordinary courage of Daniel in the lions' den.

Daniel in exile

We learn in the first three verses of chapter one that Daniel was an exile in a foreign land. King Nebuchadnezzar had overtaken Jerusalem and had required the best and the brightest from Judah to come back to Babylon and serve in his kingdom. He picked the young men who were "without any physical defect, handsome, showing aptitude for every kind of learning, well informed, quick to understand, and qualified to serve in the king's palace" (1:4). In other words, he picked people much like JBU students. Commentators suggest that Daniel was probably between the ages of thirteen to sixteen when he went into exile, when he was forced to leave the "Jerusalem bubble" of his faith and live a life of obedience in a foreign land. Now I know that there is much talk of JBU's own bubble, the spiritually sealed and protective space that encompasses the eighty acres of campus. I have always questioned whether the seal of that bubble is as tight as some seem to suggest, but there is no question on this night before graduation that, like Daniel, graduating seniors often feel as if they will be leaving this bubble and living soon in exile. How then should you live lives of obedience in exile?

Daniel as a Babylonian literature major

Notice first that Daniel learned the culture of the foreign land in which he lived. He was taught the language and literature of the Babylonians and God gave him and his friends "knowledge and understanding of all kinds of literature and learning" (Dan. 1:17). Indeed, as a professor of English, it has always been encouraging to me to recognize that Daniel and his friends were really literature majors. So, you English majors, next time that someone asks you, "What can you do with a literature major," you can respond by saying, "interpret visions and dreams" for kings, play with fire and not get burned, and pet lions without getting eaten. See what they say to that!

But seriously, I think that it is important to recognize that Daniel and his friends worked very hard to learn about the foreign culture in which they found themselves. They read and studied Scripture—Daniel is reading Jeremiah before he prays in chapter nine—but they also likely studied the Epic of Gilgamesh (remember that strange story from Masterpieces of Literature). Much of Babylonian literature was antithetical to their Jewish beliefs. It spoke of and glorified foreign gods, and it promoted "pagan" moral values. However, in God's good wisdom, Daniel and his friends needed to understand that culture in order to engage it. They needed to establish the credibility to speak by understanding the culture in which they were speaking. They also needed to discern when the foreign culture was in conflict or when it was in harmony with their faith. There is no shortcut for this hard work, and there is no excuse for not seeking to do it with excellence. When King Nebuchadnezzar gives Daniel and his friends their final exam, Scripture says, "in every matter of wisdom and understanding about which the king questioned them, he found them ten times better than all the magicians and enchanters in his whole kingdom" (1:20).

I trust that you have begun to understand the foreign culture in which you will live and work through your studies here, but I would suggest that your study is not done. Each organization and community in which you live and work will have its own distinct culture that you should understand. You will not be able to engage others as effectively in your accounting firm if you can't perform the tasks of accounting with excellence. You will not be able to engage your neighbors for Christ if you are not curious about the lives that they lead. You will not vote as intelligently without understanding the local, state, and national issues at stake. I would even suggest that you will not be able to serve in your church as effectively if you do not understand the culture outside of the church which so strongly shapes our collective desires and actions. Be lifelong learners of the culture in which you find yourself and give witness to Christ through the excellence of your work.

Daniel as a vegetarian

Of course, there is a danger in steeping yourself in the foreign culture of exile. You can easily become defined, even defiled, by that culture. Your allegiance, your worship, your identity can become so controlled by the culture that you compromise the convictions of your faith. I think that it is instructive to see how the young Daniel not only immerses himself in Babylonian culture, but also chooses to mark his identity as independent of that culture.

Daniel refuses the royal food and wine of the palace in order not to defile himself. Perhaps like me, you have always thought that Daniel was staking his identity on following the Jewish kosher food laws. However, wine is never prohibited by such laws, nor is preparation of food by Gentiles necessarily a strict prohibition. Instead, Daniel seems to be making a public choice to assert that his identity is not wholly dependent on the foreign culture. This choice seems different from the choice later in Daniel 6. It is not a choice between obeying the king and obeying God; instead it is choice to distinguish himself from the foreign culture while still functioning within the culture. Notice he is still tested by the Babylonian standard of health. As you are immersed in the exile culture, it is important sometimes to make symbolic choices to set yourself apart from the culture. Let me give you an example from my own life as a lawyer.

My practice was primarily with banks and corporations, and I was involved in a lot of large commercial transactions. Often these corporate deals involved intense periods of work—fourteen- to sixteen-hour days—for two to three weeks in a row. The culture of the firm demanded a high level of legal expertise and an unwavering commitment to serve the client. I understood that culture and sought to meet those standards while at the same time making choices to maintain independence as a follower of Christ. It was not easy.

One public choice that I made early was to let people know that I was in church on Sunday mornings, so not available for meetings. It may not sound like much—perhaps like eating vegetarian food in a Babylonian palace—but it became an important marker for me and for others. For instance, in December of my second year, I was involved in a deal that was supposed to close before January 1. All of the parties decided to come to our offices the day after Christmas and work literally day and night until we finished the transaction. I saw the conflict looming as Sunday fell just two days before January 1. I am not, nor was I, legalistic about Sunday worship: my salvation was not at stake if I missed church, but I also knew that Sunday worship had been a marker for me of who I was beyond the law firm and that others had noticed. I did not know how much they had noticed until 2:00 AM on Saturday night/Sunday morning when the lead partner, a nonreligious person, came into my office and looked surprised to see me. He smiled a wry, almost wistful, smile as he told me that I better get home to clean up before church and that he would see me again at noon. It was a smile that conveyed a longing for an identity grounded in something beyond the culture of professional achievement in the law firm.

You should decide how you will mark your identity as separate from the culture in which you operate. It may be through hosting a Bible study at lunch, or volunteering with the food kitchen at your church, or taking care of your dying mother, or it may be where you choose to live, or how you commute to work, or how you treat your co-workers. It will, no matter what, involve how you explain the motivation for your choice, not by a dictating of legalistic rules but by marking a different allegiance to the God whom you serve. It will be a testimony to others but it will also be a way for you to remain faithful to your calling as a child of God living in exile.

Daniel had good friends.

Daniel had good friends—Shadrach, Meshack, and Abendego—upon whom he relied to live out a life of faith in exile. They trained together; they ate together; they worked together; and they prayed together. In chapter 2, when King Nebuchadnezzar asked for his wise men to tell him his dream and then interpret it or else be killed, Daniel seeks out his friends, Shadrach, Meshack, and Abednego, and "urged them to plead for mercy from the God of heaven concerning this mystery" (Dan.

2:18). God answers their collective prayer by revealing the king's dream to Daniel. Daniel is rewarded by the king by being "placed . . . in a high position"(Dan. 2:48), making him in charge of all the wise men. Daniel responds by putting his friends in charge under him. He trusts them because he knows their true allegiance to God.

You too will need good friends to help you to continue to live out your life of faith. And finding such good friends may well be more difficult when you leave college. They will not be around the corner in a residence hall, throwing a Frisbee on the quad, across the aisle in the classroom, or working with you in the lab. You will find these friends at work, in your neighborhood, and at your church. You may even find them in your own family, and dare I say it, even your own parents may become friends. And, if God calls you to marry, I trust that you and your spouse will share a deep friendship. Look for these friends and put yourself in a position to rely on them to encourage you to faithfulness.

Daniel prays and worships.

Finally, we should notice that Daniel and his friends were people who lived lives of confidence because they knew whom they served. They were ready for the big moment because they knew God through the ordinary moments of worship and prayer. Shadrach, Meshack, and Abednego refuse to bow and worship the king because they worshiped the true King. Listen to their confidence when they confront the king: "O Nebuchadnezzar, we do not need to defend ourselves before you in this matter. If we are thrown into the blazing furnace, the God we serve is able to save us from it, and he will rescue us from your hand, O king" (3:16-17). And here are their best lines: "But even if he does not, we want you to know, O king, that we will not serve your gods or worship the image of gold you have set up" (3:18).

Daniel learns of the decree to pray only to Darius, and he confidently walks home and opens the windows facing Jerusalem and prays to the true God. Scripture tells us that prayer is a habit in Daniel's life: "three times a day he got down on his knees and prayed, giving thanks to his God, just as he had done before." Just as he had done before—simple words that speak of a life of ordinary obedience. Daniel and his friends are ready for the big thing because they have lived a life of faithful obedience in the little things.

We really have only one task in life: that is, to become more and more faithful followers of Jesus Christ. That is the one big thing that should orient our lives; that is the one vision that should guide our choices. In following Christ, we may be led into a burning furnace or a den of lions; we may be called to serve those with cancer, create jobs for those in the city, open our home to a single mother, design more energy-efficient buildings, heal the sick, give sight to the blind, or love the lonely. We are called to many great things as followers of Jesus Christ, but we won't be ready to hear or respond to that call if we have not developed habits of ordinary obedience to follow him. So I suggest that you continue to understand the culture in which you live, that you continue to choose to be different, that you continue to rely on friends who follow Christ, and that you continue to seek the face of the one true God in worship and prayer.

May it always be true of us.

CHAPTER 5

The Baccalaureate Service

Saying Farewell

The first baccalaureate service occurred in Oxford in 1432 when Oxford graduates were required for the first time by statute to give a sermon in Latin as part of their final academic exercises before commencement. Baccalaureate services have had a rich history ever since, including in higher education in the United States. Harvard has had a baccalaureate service since its first commencement in 1642, and many colleges and universities such as Yale, Dartmouth, Columbia, Bates, and Tufts continue the practice today. Historically, the baccalaureate service is more of a worship service in comparison to the graduation ceremony, more of a giving of thanks to God for years of learning and wisdom than a celebration of an academic achievement. The contemporary baccalaureate services in private, secular institutions still retain some religious aspect, but almost always now reflect their very diverse, interfaith contexts. Typically, the president or perhaps a university minister or the dean, speaks and offers his or her final words of advice to the graduating seniors, advice that tends to call students to remain curious about ideas, to take risks professionally, to serve others freely, and to remain loyal to their alma mater. The service also often includes music and speech performances by students.

When I came to JBU, we added a baccalaureate service on the Friday evening before the spring commencement service on Saturday. I thought that it was important to include a formal time of worship in the commencement weekend so that we might recognize together Christ as the source of our learning and calling. I also wanted a final opportunity to speak to the graduating seniors before they left, a time not only to say good-bye, but also to encourage them in their obedience to God's call on their lives after their time at the university. We also include music and a short speech from a graduating senior in our service, so other than the speaking in Latin, it truly is a revival of the traditional baccalaureate service and an apt way for students to begin to imagine the rest of their lives following graduation.

Strangers in the World

Text: 1 Peter 1:1-2

Peter, an apostle of Jesus Christ, to God's elect, strangers in the world, scattered throughout Pontus, Galatia, Cappadocia, Asia and Bithynia, who have been chosen according to the foreknowledge of God the Father through the sanctifying work of the Spirit, for obedience to Jesus Christ and sprinkling by his blood:

    Grace and peace be yours in abundance.

Our passage is the opening lines of 1 Peter. It is technically called the salutation, the opening greeting that is traditionally part of a first-century letter. We too have our salutations that take on a ritual form; for instance, there is the salute of the soldier to his or her commanding officer, or there is the standard greeting of my children to their friends on Instant Messenger—"hey" or "wus up." There is also the greeting of one JBU professor to another: "Hello, how are you?" Indeed, one of the more interesting parts of my job is to watch students experiment with ways to greet me. I have heard everything from "Hi, Chipper," to "Good morning, Mr. President."

Salutations are by their very nature at the beginning of the conversation, so you may wonder why I chose a scriptural salutation as the text for this final baccalaureate address. It is because this whole commencement weekend is a strange ritual. It operates with the assumption that commencement is more about the beginning of a new life rather than the ending of an old one, more of a focus on the future rather than on the past. Accordingly, a scriptural salutation seems to me to be exactly the right text to look at for this baccalaureate service as we consider the beginning of your new life after JBU.

While these two verses are rich with theological implication, I want to focus on three phrases: two that set out the challenge of the Christian life, particularly perhaps the challenge of your Christian life following college, and one that identifies the means of support that Christ provides to meet that challenge. First, let us look at the challenges.

"God's elect, strangers in the world, scattered throughout"

Peter addresses his letter to "God's elect, strangers in the world, scattered throughout" Asia. There are three separate ideas here: being God's chosen people, being a stranger in this world, and being scattered. Let's look at them in reverse order. Peter identifies his audience as "scattered" throughout Asia Minor. Indeed, the Greek word for this scattering is *diaspora*, and it is used here as a literal description of the Jewish Christians who are scattered away from the center of their world, which had been Jerusalem. This experience of *diaspora*, of being scattered, is a central one in the biblical narrative and in the Christian life. It is in the exile of God's people to Egypt and later to Babylon; it is central to Jeremiah; and it is a part of the Great Commission when Christ calls us to "make disciples of all the nations." *Diaspora* is part of the imparting of the Holy Spirit when Christ challenges us to be "witnesses in Jerusalem, and in all Judea and Samaria, and to the ends of the earth" (Acts 1:8), and part of the experience of God's people throughout history when through either missions or persecution God has moved his people to scatter across the world.

It is difficult to be asked to be scattered because it involves leaving home, family, and friends. Indeed, I expect that this graduation weekend is bittersweet for many of you: sweet because it marks the completion of a major accomplishment, but bitter because you recognize that you will be "scattered" all over the world after this weekend. No matter how hard we try in our alumni office, we will never be able to gather you altogether again at any single event. Moreover, the scattering of this weekend will likely be repeated in your life. The post office tells us that fifteen percent of the United States population changes addresses every year. Census data suggests that the average American will move eleven times in his or her lifetime. Scattering will be a part of your life, and it is often a part of God's plan to ask us to scatter: to set us in new contexts for new realms of service, to establish new friendships that will encourage spiritual growth, and to make us more reliant on God and less reliant on ourselves. Indeed, Peter ties this process of being scattered, of moving, of being a part of a *diaspora*, with his description of our true state in this world, the second phrase of his challenge. We are strangers in this world.

Other translations of this phrase give us a fuller range of meanings. We are "sojourners," "pilgrims," "exiles," or even "refugees," those who live as foreigners. Each of these terms conveys a good sense of the unease and transitory nature of a Christian's life in this world. We are not fully at home here, nor should we be. Indeed, many of you have had this experience of living as a stranger in a different country during your four, five, or six years here at college. Some of you came to JBU from other countries, and you experienced being a "stranger" in Siloam Springs, learning the ways of North American college culture and the customs of McDonalds and Walmart, for the first time. Others of you have gone to Northern Ireland, France, Britain, Guatemala, Ethiopia, or some country that is foreign to your United States upbringing and have lived there as a stranger. My family and I have also experienced this life of being strangers, having twice lived in England for extended periods of time. These cross-cultural experiences help us to understand better the dynamic of living as Christians, as strangers scattered in this world.

Studies show that people often follow a similar emotional pattern in their experience of living as strangers, a pattern described as culture shock. You typically experience a sense of elation in the first three or four weeks in a new place. You are a tourist on vacation and you enjoy the newness of your surrounding and the freedom of travel. You notice the difference between the foreign culture and your own culture, and you tend to find these differences endearing. For instance, during the first couple of weeks when my family lived in England, we enjoyed fish and chips in paper-wrappers, reading the newspaper accounts of football (soccer) matches, drinking tea and chocolate-covered biscuits (cookies), and the deep green landscape.

However, after a month, the differences in the culture are no longer endearing; they are annoying at best and deeply unsettling at worst. I remember distinctly that after four weeks of living in England, our family had a complete meltdown on a Sunday afternoon. The kids complained about walking so much and the awful food and they cried about missing their friends. We were all tired of trying to decipher the English accent and understand people in conversation. The weather was cold and rainy, and the beds were lumpy and hard. We were a mess, but it was a normal emotional trough in the cycle of learning to live as strangers in another country. Typically that pattern of elation and depression is repeated at least once more before a person "adapts" or reaches the stage described as biculturalism: the ability to function in two cultures with confidence, always recognizing one's home culture as the source of one's identity but actively and fully engaging the foreign culture as well.

I would like to suggest that this process should characterize how we as Christians live in the world but not of the world. Now, not every-one moves through this cycle to biculturalism: some get stuck in the troughs. They suffer what experts call "culture shock," the symptoms of which you should perhaps be aware as you are about to leave college so that you can diagnose yourself in September. The symptoms of "culture shock" include feelings of anxiety, homesickness, helplessness, boredom, depression, confusion, self-doubt, feelings of inadequacy, unexplained fits of weeping, paranoia, psychosomatic illnesses. This list may well sound familiar because it may characterize your freshman experience.

When people experience culture shock, they often withdraw from the new cross-cultural experiences; they tend to hang out only with people from their own country, avoid contact with residents of the host nation; and have a deep desire to quit and return home. Alternately, they decide to stay but permanently hate the country and its people—a sort of grin-and-bear-it approach.

Christians can, and in many ways should, feel a sense of disequilibrium as they function in this world. We are strangers in this world; however, we must not let the culture shock of functioning as strangers lead us to a point of complete withdrawal from this world, a withdrawal that is a real and present danger in our Christian subculture. Indeed, it is one of my great challenges in working at a Christian university because it is so easy to withdraw. It is also a temptation that you may face as you experience the culture shock of leaving JBU. We can withdraw from the world to the point that we have little to no interaction with non-Christians. We can withdraw to the point that we just reject the culture and its people instead of seeking to redeem them. We can also withdraw to the point that we consider this life as just something to grin and bear until we get to heaven. However, I think that we are not fully living as God's strangers in this world if we just reject the people and culture in which we find ourselves and withdraw. Instead, we should work to become bicultural, recognizing that our identity must be grounded in our Christian faith but also having the confidence to engage our culture and its people to bring about God's good in this world.

You "who have been chosen"

Okay, I know that this is not sounding like the most upbeat message for graduation weekend: "Congratulations, you will now become strangers scattered throughout this world." What gives us the confidence to face such a challenge? As Peter suggests in these two verses, your confidence comes from the knowledge that you are child of God. As it says in this passage, you are chosen by God, sanctified by the Holy Spirit, "for obedience to Christ and sprinkling by his blood." You are equipped to be strangers scattered throughout this world only to the extent that you know who you are and to whom you belong. As Paul says in 1 Corinthians, "You are not your own; you were bought at a price" (6:19-20). As you leave this place and you become again and again strangers scattered throughout the world, you must each remember that you are a beloved child of God. It is only by relying on your identity in Christ that you can have the confidence to function as a bicultural stranger in this world.

Perhaps a story can help illustrate this point. When my second son, Ben, was just turning two, I was practicing law in Chicago. It was the Christmas season, and I was involved in a huge corporate deal. It had to be finished by January 1, and I worked every day but Christmas for twelve to fourteen hours a day during those final two weeks. We completed the deal on December 31, so I was able to be home on New Years' Day. Now, obviously, my kids had not seen me much during those two weeks, and I was feeling a bit of parental guilt, particularly about my older son who was five at the time. I didn't think that Ben, again only two years of age, was old enough to have missed me. We spent the morning playing around with their new Christmas gifts, and then, in the afternoon, I began to clean up some of the holiday mess and started to head to the front door. Ben came toddling around the corner just as I opened the door, and he started crying. He reached out to me, stamped his foot in anger, and started shouting at me, "My Daddy, My Daddy!" I, of course, swept him up in my arms and gave him a big hug and the assurance that I wasn't leaving. Ben is currently fifteen, and I know that now he would be more likely to open the door and gently escort me out of the house; however, his two-year-old response touched me deeply. My absence had clearly made Ben feel alienated and alone, a stranger scattered in this world, and he responded by claiming his rights as my child. I would encourage you to do the same as you experience this sense of estrangement, this culture shock of living in the world but not of the world. Do not be afraid to reach out your hand, stamp your foot, and claim your right as a child of God. Claim your identity in Christ, call out for "My Daddy, My Daddy."

Indeed, some of you may have never responded to God's call on your life, never claimed the privilege of becoming a child of God, and you face a much deeper estrangement than being a stranger in this world. You are estranged from the living God. However, we preach good news, for Christ stands ready to receive you; and when you call on him, you will be calling to one, who, unlike me with my son Ben, will never be absent, never slumber, and never sleep.

"Grace and peace will be yours in abundance."

What will be the fruits of relying on your identity in Christ? The end of the passage answers that question: grace and peace will be yours in abundance. Grace is God's favor, kindness, friendship, his acceptance and love, which we can do nothing to earn or deserve. Peace is a sense of wholeness, completeness, and well-being that comes from a dependence on God. Here then is the paradox of Peter's salutation, indeed it is the paradox of the Christian life; even as we are called to live as strangers scattered throughout this world, we are the children of the King, and his grace and peace will be ours in abundance. May you also find it so and may God bless you with his grace and peace in abundance.

May it always be true of us.

Living in Exile

Text: Isaiah 40:27-31

Why do you say, O Jacob, and complain, O Israel, "My way is hidden from the LORD; my cause is disregarded by my God"? Do you not know? Have you not heard? The LORD is the everlasting God, the Creator of the ends of the earth. He will not grow tired or weary, and his understanding no one can fathom. He gives strength to the weary and increases the power of the weak. Even youths grow tired and weary, and young men stumble and fall; but those who hope in the LORD will renew their strength. They will soar on wings like eagles; they will run and not grow weary, they will walk and not be faint.

When Carey and I lived in Charlottesville, Virginia, we attended a small, evangelical Anglican church of about 125 people. It was a church that preached the Word both from the pulpit and through its liturgy. We were actively involved in the church, teaching Sunday school and leading the youth group. One Sunday, the rector mentioned that the bishop was coming and asked us whether we wanted to become members, which in this church tradition meant being confirmed. Now Carey and I had always been actively involved in church, but we had never officially joined one, not as a matter of principle, but because we were rarely in a place for more than two or three years in the first part of our marriage and many of those churches did not have a formal membership expectation. We agreed to attend the confirmation classes, and decided to join this church formally by proclaiming our faith publicly in the confirmation service. As part of our class, we were instructed that we would come before the bishop who would gently slap us on the face, lay his hand on our head, and speak the prayer of confirmation. Now I understood all of these practices except this slapping of the face business. It sounded a bit harsh, even abusive, in a service in which I was publicly confirming my faith in Christ. The rector explained that the slap was a symbolic reminder to the person being confirmed that living in this world will be hard at times, that even as Christians we should expect that it will be difficult. In other words, the slap was an important part of the trajectory of the service, a reminder of trouble along with an affirmation of faith in Christ. It was a liturgy that embodied the truth of John 16:33: "In this world you will have trouble. But take heart! I have overcome the world."

I have never forgotten that slap, and, at the risk of being a really depressing speaker tonight, I have envisioned this sermon as sort of that symbolic slap before we head into the celebration of graduation tomorrow. I offer this symbolic slap, not because I want to dampen the celebration, but because I want to deepen it. I believe that one of the most important things that we can teach you at JBU is how to be spiritually resilient in the face of life's troubles, a resiliency that comes not only from the skills, talents, and knowledge that you have acquired here, but also because you have come to know God and you have learned to wait expectantly for him.

I want to look at selected passages from Isaiah 40 to help us understand the source of this spiritual resiliency. We need a little context to understand Isaiah 40 because it begins a new section of the book. In the first thirty-nine chapters, Isaiah has been prophesying the downfall and forced migration of the people of Jerusalem and Judah. In chapters 40–55, those earlier prophesies have come to fulfillment, and the writer is speaking from the perspective of the people in exile in Babylon.

What is the life of the person in exile? Many of you know something of that experience of exile in coming to JBU from around the world and even from different parts of the country. You have felt the loneliness and alienation of living in a place that is not your home. The food is different—barbecue not black beans. The landscape is different—rolling hills and chicken farms instead of plains filled with wheat or suburbs filled with houses. The climate is different—hot August days and one day of snow in February instead of months of cold or the ocean breezes. The local customs are different—I still can't call the hogs nor have I quite figured out what a razorback is. When you are in exile, you are constantly reminded that you are not at home.

As people of faith, we are people in exile, people who are called to do kingdom work in this world but also people who are not completely at home in this world. Sin has bent this world and our lives in it. We know of this brokenness and alienation even here at JBU. It is in the telephone call from home about the death of a grandparent. It is in the unkind words of the roommate whom you thought was your friend. It is in the boredom that cannot be filled by music, or video games, or movies. It is in the depression that consumes your days in the darkness that you cannot light. It is in the uncertainty that terrorism, or global markets, or natural disasters might sweep you up and crush your future. It is in the ache of loneliness that you feel even in a crowd or at church. It is in the nagging fear that even tonight, on the eve of your graduation and after four or five years of college you are still not sure what God would have you do in this world. Don't worry—he has many things for you to do and you have already been doing them. Moreover, and this may be the moment when the slap in the face stings the most, it is in the recognition that the fears and troubles of living in a sin-sick world will never go away; humans have lived in exile ever since leaving the garden, and our experience in the exile has been filled with trouble.

The natural response to this never-ending trouble is complaint. "God does not care for me. I have been forgotten. I don't understand why these things are happening to me. Why do evil people prosper and my way seems to fail?" Perhaps there are even questions of whether God exists or whether he has the power to change circumstances. Indeed, it is a complaint that is expressed in Isaiah 40:27: "Why do you say, O Jacob, and complain, O Israel, 'My way is hidden from the LORD; my cause is disregarded by my God?'" It is the common grievance against God when life is difficult. Indeed, it is the reasonable human perspective to living in a sinful world. But the prophet responds incredulously with questions: "Do you not know? Have you not heard?" You can almost hear the disbelief in his voice. And then he gives his readers four important characteristics about the nature of God.

God is the God of the long view.

First, the prophet tells us that the Lord is the everlasting God, or in another translation, Yahweh is a God of the long view, which is a great description of God. He accomplishes his purposes over the long haul. He measures results over a lifetime, not over a semester or even four years. He sees the trajectory of your life and he understands how this particular trouble fits into that trajectory. We should take comfort in knowing that God has a long view and try to emulate that view when we face difficulties.

God is the God of the borderlands.

The prophet also describes God as the Creator of the ends of the earth, or in my alternative version, Creator of the borderlands. If the first characteristic, that God has a long-term perspective on life, works with a metaphor of time, then this metaphor is about space. There is nowhere that God is not involved because he has literally created the borders of life. Indeed, the power and majesty of God's creation is depicted throughout Isaiah 40. The prophet talks of God as one who "measured the waters in the hollow of his hand" and "marked off the heavens" with his hand (40:12). He is the one who "held the dust of the earth in a basket" and "weighed the mountains on the scales" (40:12). He is the one who "brings out the starry host one by one, and calls them each by name. Because of his great power and mighty strength, not one of them

197

is missing" (40:26). We serve the God who created the very borderlands of existence.

God is the God who does not grow tired or weary.

The prophet also tells us that God does not grow tired or weary. Again, God is sufficient where we are weak. Sleep is one of the first things affected when a person is experiencing emotional or physical hardship. Indeed, it is often one of the doctor's first questions—how are you sleeping? And, if you have been through a period of stress or illness, you know how it affects your sleeping. You wake up thinking about the problem and cannot get back to sleep. Then you become stressed about not sleeping, which makes the situation worse. Some of the worst times are actually in the middle of the night when you are awake alone and you can't stop worrying. Moreover, there is a cumulative effect to that stress: the lack of sleep and the constant worry or physical hardship makes you weary and tired during the day. However, we serve a God who does not grow tired or weary. He cares for you even in the middle of the night because he neither slumbers nor sleeps. Shakespeare, in *Macbeth*, says that "sleep knits up the ragged sleeve of time," but our God does not need to be knit up; he does not need to be restored; instead, he is the restorer.

God's understanding is beyond us.

Finally, the prophet tells us no one can fathom or probe God's understanding: God's mind is not our mind. As the prophet writes in verses 13-14, "Who has understood the mind of the LORD, or instructed him as his counselor? Whom did the LORD consult to enlighten him, and who taught him the right way? Who was it that taught him knowledge or showed him the path of understanding?" Of course, this truth about God's character is one of the hardest to accept when we are facing life's difficulties because we want God to explain to us the purposes of our suffering. We want to have God's understanding of the stillborn child, the devastation of tsunamis in Asia or hurricanes in Louisiana, the millions of AIDS victims in Africa, the invisible children who are kidnapped to become soldiers in Uganda, the divorce of our parents, or of the rejection of our friends. And the prophet rightly reminds us that we will never fully probe the understanding of God. We can never fully have his perspective, and often we may not have answers to our questions of suffering. We must trust God in these times of difficulty.

And why should we trust? Who is this God that we should trust in him? Certainly, he is the God of the long view, the God who created the ends of the earth, the God who never grows tired or weary, the God whose understanding is never probed, but the prophet tells us in Isaiah 40 that he is more. Our God offers comfort, he speaks tenderly to our hearts, and he promises us that our "sin has been paid for." The prophet tells us that "the word of our God stands forever" (40:8). Our God is also strong and gentle; he protects us with his mighty arm but he also "gathers the lambs in his arms and carries them close to his heart; he gently leads those that have young" (40:11). Our God is greater than all political structures ("before him all nations are as nothing"—40:17) and more powerful than any political leader ("he brings princes to naught and reduces the rulers of this world to nothing"—40:23). And what do we receive if we decide to trust in our God? Listen to the final glorious verses of the chapter: "Even youths grow tired and weary, and young men stumble and fall, but those who hope in the LORD [or, alternatively translated, "those who wait expectantly on the LORD"] they will renew their strength; they will soar on wings like eagles, they will run and not grow weary, they will walk and not be faint."

That is spiritual resiliency when we choose to wait expectantly on the Lord even when we are tired and weary. The image of the eagle soaring on the thermal updrafts is a good one. The eagle sets itself into a position to take advantage of the natural power provided by God; it does not exert a lot of its own energy flapping its wings. It trusts in what God provides. Similarly, when you face difficulties in life, put yourself into a position to wait expectantly on what God provides. Put your faith in the truth that God will be sufficient for all circumstances; put your faith in the truth of God's character. And God promises to renew your strength. It is that promise to which you should cling in times of difficulty.

Now, I have to admit something to you. Sometimes young presidents grow tired and weary, sometimes young presidents stumble and fall. Sometimes the difficulties of life and the job seem a bit too much. You worry about the students hurting themselves as they climb 150 feet up the radio tower or on top of the cathedral to hang a black flag. You agonize to set tuition rates so that families can afford to come and so that you can pay people fairly. You ache in making the decision to ask a student to be gone for a semester or not to renew a contract. You are saddened by the news of a marriage falling apart. You are distressed to hear that a faculty member has had a heart attack. You are frustrated by criticism of "the administration" but you know that it is not right to share all of the facts to defend yourself. And, then, you hear that your brother-in-law has bone cancer and may not live out the rest of the year. Sometimes you want to cry out—in the words of the Negro spiritual—"ease up, Lord." So, as you see, I preach as much to myself as I do to you today. I too stand with you in need to hear the words of the prophet, to know that those who hope in the Lord will renew their strength. They will soar on wings like eagles; they will run and not grow weary; they walk and not be faint.

And you know what? God does renew your strength. He does give you encouragement in times of difficulties. He does increase the power of the weak. And, as university president, God often renews my strength through notes from students like you. Let me read you part of a note that I received last week.

I wanted to thank you once more about speaking last night, but I also wanted to share something with you as well. I am not in the habit of sharing personal things in emails, but it is something that I felt was on my heart as I was praying this morning. When I came here I was a person that was struggling to justify living an ungodly lifestyle while still being a Christian. I had my life compartmentalized: in one box I had my Christian ideals, and in another box I had the way I actually lived my life. This is where I entered my walk when I came to JBU.

Over my years here I started to meet students, professors, speakers, etc. who were unlike most of the Christians that I was used to: their Christian walk was personal and their faith was actually tangible. This challenged me, made me question life and my perception of it. Eventually it had me turn back to the Bible and meditate on Scripture to try to comprehend the effect people's Christian walk had on their lives. I turned to God and he started to redefine my faith. I started to grow spiritually in a way I had never experienced and led to many things, from getting actively involved with a Church, helping start a student ministry, as well as redefining how I needed to change to best be a servant.

After reading this you might be wondering what my ramblings have to do with you, since it is you whom I am addressing. I would like to thank you. . . . [and then he says a few personal things about me before ending.] I came in as one of those wounded souls, and am leaving here as a person solidified in Christ; weak in my own nature but strengthened beyond my limitations by God's presence. Thank you.

P.S.—Please try to overlook the grammar in this letter; I'm sure the English teacher in you will want to hand this back to me bleeding with red ink.

Such notes renew my strength because God uses them to remind me that it is working here for many of you at JBU: we are granting you a diploma tomorrow to credential your fine academic work over the last four years, but we have also been passing along the faith to you, however imperfectly and partially, in the academic, spiritual, residential, and social programs at JBU. I will raucously celebrate your academic achievement tomorrow, but I am also quietly grateful for the many evidences of your deepening spiritual resilience—both bring me great encouragement.

We should return for a moment to that confirmation service. While I have spent most of our time talking about the "slap in the face," the service does not, of course, end there. The bishop goes on to lay his hands on the person's head and then pray for God to keep and preserve that person in the faith. Quite literally the bishop lays hands on the next generation of Christians who need the spiritual resiliency to carry on the faith. Now I am not a bishop and there is no way that I can touch each of your heads, but I do think that it would be appropriate to end this talk by asking the God of long view, the God of the ends of the earth, the God who never grows tired or weary, the God whose ways we cannot fathom, to bless and keep you as you leave JBU—to give you spiritual resilience as you go out to serve his kingdom. Will you join me in prayer?

"Defend, O Lord, these thy servants with thy heavenly grace, that they may continue to be thine for ever; and that they daily increase in thy Holy Spirit more and more, until they come unto thy everlasting kingdom."

May it always be true of us.

And Hope Will Not Disappoint Us

Text: Romans 5:2-5

And we rejoice in the hope of the glory of God. Not only so, but we also rejoice in our sufferings, because we know that suffering produces perseverance; perseverance, character; and character, hope. And hope does not disappoint us, because God has poured out his love into our hearts by the Holy Spirit, whom he has given us.

Congratulations! You have made it. You are graduating tomorrow. Most of you (and I) came to JBU together four years ago, but now you will be leaving whereas I am being held back for another year (at least that is what the Board of Trustees told me a couple of weeks ago). One of you pointed this out to me this week in an email note. Let me read a bit of it.

Dear President Pollard,

It is 3:30 A.M. I know . . . I know . . . I should be sleeping especially because I have an exam at 8 A.M., but I have been having something in the back of my head this week!

This coming Saturday, May 3, I will be graduating from this fantastic institution but to be completely honest with you it will be hard to leave. Do you remember when we came 4 years ago? We (including you) came full of dreams, expectations, and a few tears and doubts. I am pretty sure that just like you, I did not know what I was getting into. Four years later one thing has remained, the Lord has continued to guide our steps. In my case with my classes, relationships and opportunities, you through your relations with alumni, raising funds, and trying to make JBU a better place for us.

In a way you are graduating too! Your freshman class is graduating and you are pretty well accepted among the senior community. There is only one little thing that I do not like, you get to stay, I have to leave. Because of this reason I have one request for the many years you have left here at JBU. Please take care of my school. I know its a joint effort, running this school is not completely up to you. But I think I can get around with this one because I am pretty sure you love this place as much as I do.

I won't lie. I have some tears in my eyes. Although do not worry, most of them are tears of joy. Those dreams and expectations were surpassed, those tears and doubts were overcome. President Pollard, remember that you will never walk alone, you have a student body that respects you and a staff that supports you, but above else a Father in heaven who will guide all your steps.

When I get notes like this, I really do think that I have one of the best jobs in the world.

Our passage in Romans helps to explain the significance of joy and suffering in the Christian life and serves as a hinge in Paul's letter, serving as a summary of what he says in the first five chapters and then pointing toward what he wants to talk about in the next three chapters. Paul begins by summarizing the results of our justification through faith: we have peace with God; we stand in the grace of God; and we hope in the glory of God. The peace is immediate, the grace is continuing, and the glory is expected. In particular, notice Paul's claim that we rejoice, or in other translations, we "boast" in the hope in the glory of God. As John Stott, author of *Men Made New* suggests, our hope here is our certain confidence that we will be with God in his glory in heaven; it is our confidence in the ultimate results of justification, a sharing in God's glory.

However, then Paul immediately goes on to suggest that we also should rejoice, or "boast," in our suffering. Paul is not willing for us to simply sit back and wait for the future glory of heaven. He also recognizes that we have to live in this world, and this world can be a world of suffering. But isn't it a strange suggestion to ask us to rejoice in suffering? Christians are not masochists, people who find pleasure in pain; nor are we stoics, people who just endure pain. Instead, Paul suggests that we should rejoice in our suffering because we recognize the results that suffering can bring in our lives, suffering that will lead us to deepen our hope in the glory of God. Paul spells out those results through employing an ancient rhetorical device called a concatenation or *gradatio*, a linking of terms to suggest a logical progression. Suffering produces perseverance; perseverance, character; and character, hope. Let's take a look at each of those terms in turn.

"Suffering"

Suffering is the hardship of living in a world broken by sin. In Romans 8, Paul speaks of suffering in terms of troubles, hardship, persecution, famine, nakedness, danger, or violence. Many of you know something of suffering, either directly in your own life or in the lives of those whom you have served. Indeed, even though it does not seem quite right to say this today before the celebration of graduation, I do trust that you have suffered some during your time here at JBU. I trust that you have had some difficult relationships with people, that you have been challenged to study beyond what you ever thought possible, that you have been overwhelmed at times by the needs in your own life and the lives of others. You have had times of doubt or discouragement, been lonely and uncertain, and been confronted by injustice or unfairness. When prospective parents ask me what they can do best for their children as they come to college, I often answer by saying, "Let them struggle a bit. Don't save them from every problem." I hope that you have had trouble in your time at JBU because it is through this trouble that you develop perseverance.

"Perseverance"

As Paul suggests, suffering produces perseverance. Perseverance, endurance, steadfastness, resolve, resilience—these are attributes that we need when we face the inevitable sufferings that will come our way. When conflict begins to emerge in your marriage, you do not look for an easy way out, but you hang on and seek help. When you face a challenging boss, you do not quickly seek another job, but you renew your commitment to serve him or her. When you cannot at first find an answer in the laboratory, you do not just move on to an easier project, but you try a new method. When you experience quarrels in your church, you do not simply look for a new church down the road, but you act as a peacemaker. When you see injustice, you do not just ignore it, but you try to fix it. You choose, in other words, to persevere despite the suffering because you know that the suffering will build your character. As you choose again and again to work through the suffering, you begin to develop habits of being, routines of living that define your identity. You become a certain type of person. As Paul says, suffering produces perseverance, and perseverance, character.

"Character"

Paul's term "character" could also be translated as tested character, or tested genuineness, or even authenticity. Now I have spent enough time with students your age to know that you deeply value authenticity, honesty, transparency, realness, and you can be skeptical of marketing, hype, polished performance, and of anything corporate. Many of you like the neighborhood coffee shop better than Starbucks; you listen to music from indie bands rather than from major recording artists; you are more interested in Youtube videos that are grainy and made by your friends than you are in movies in the theater. You may also be drawn to alternative churches that meet in coffee houses rather than the megachurch in a corporate building, and you certainly are skeptical of guys who wear ties like your president. You want to live authentic, honest, and real lives, and I applaud you for that desire. However, Paul suggests that you develop that authentic or genuine character more through suffering than through skepticism of marketing, more through perseverance than through spontaneity or informality, more through choosing habits of being in this troubled world than through where you choose to drink your coffee. I urge you to become people of true, tested genuineness, of proven character, of biblical authenticity by recognizing that suffering produces perseverance; perseverance, character; and character, hope.

"Hope"

As followers of Christ, we should be a people of hope, a people who have a confident expectation that all will come out right despite the suffering of this broken world. As Julian of Norwich writes, "All shall be well / And all shall be well / And all manner of things shall be well." We are a people of hope, not primarily because of our own efforts to persevere in suffering until we develop a genuine character, but because we follow Christ, the God who is acquainted with grief but steadfast in his love for us. In other words, we hope not in ourselves, but in Christ, and so, as Paul writes, we know that "hope does not disappoint us because God has poured out his love into our hearts by the Holy Spirit, whom he has given us."

Even though I have spent the better part of ten minutes explaining this passage to you, I think that you already know the truth of it. I think this because of the ways in which you have responded to speakers in chapel. I believe that there have been only two outside chapel speakers in the last four years in which the student body has responded with a spontaneous standing ovation at the end of chapel. Do you remember for whom you stood and applauded?

Both of these speakers were older women—well into their seventies. Both of them were slight of build—probably not more than a hundred pounds. Both of them spoke using only their voice and the Bible—no digital presentation, no fancy PowerPoint, no animated gestures, and no funny speaker stories. I hate to admit it now, but when I heard that each of these women were coming to speak, I worried that they were going to bomb, that they would not "relate" to young people because they were too old. So I confess to you today, not only my sin of age discrimination, but also my stupidity in thinking I knew whom God would use to speak to you. I am sure glad that I am not the campus pastor at JBU. Both of them spoke of suffering, a suffering that produces perseverance; perseverance, character; and character, hope. And both of them bore witness that such "hope does not disappoint us, because God has poured out his love into our hearts by the Holy Spirit, whom he has given us."

You gave one of those standing ovations to Jill Briscoe during her first visit here when she spoke to us of her work with the suffering church in Vietnam and China. She spoke of the deep hunger of the church in those countries for biblical instruction and the great risk and danger that people took to hear God's words preached. She spoke from the proven authenticity of a life in which she was still taking risks to be with those who suffered. Indeed, she told us that she focuses all of her time now on either speaking with the persecuted church around the world or with young people in the United States and England, hoping the next generation would be inspired to preach that hope that does not disappoint us.

The second ovation was for Alexandre Goode, the grandmother of several of our students. She told us of how as an orphan teenager in Russia, she was caught up in the Nazi death camps. She spoke of her great suffering in the camps, painful hunger, unspeakable violence, punishing work, sexual abuse, and of despair. She also told us of how

Christ made himself manifest to her in the camps and how she came to faith through that suffering. She recalled her miraculous escape from a transport train and her liberation by the allied forces. She then spoke of her recovery and of how the doctors predicted that she would never be able to have children because of the injuries that she sustained. Then, do you remember, with a glint in her eye and a grin on her face, she spoke of her hope in the God of miracles, her hope in a God who had given her three children and over fifteen grandchildren, her hope in a God that did not disappoint her. Moreover, she too has not retired from doing God's work. She and her husband still run an adoption agency to place Russian children with disabilities in homes in the United States. Mrs. Goode also bore witness with her life to the suffering that produces perseverance; perseverance, character; and character, hope. And you recognized that truth of that witness with your ovation.

Graduating students, my hope for you is that you too will continue to develop a tested character that gives witness to a hope that will not disappoint, that you too will develop a resilient identity in Christ that testifies to God's love poured in your hearts by the Holy Spirit. God may not call you to as dramatic an engagement with the suffering of this world as preaching to the persecuted church or surviving the Holocaust, but you will be called to engage with suffering in your own life and the lives of others, and, God willing, you too can rejoice in that suffering because suffering produces perseverance; perseverance, character; and character, hope.

May it always be true of us.

Establish the Work of Our Hands

Text: Psalm 90 (ESV)

A Prayer of Moses, the Man of God

Lord you have been our dwelling place in all generations.

Before the mountains were brought forth, or ever you had formed the earth and the world, from everlasting to everlasting you are God.

You return man to dust and say, "Return, O children of man!"

For a thousand years in your sight are but as yesterday when it is past, or as a watch in the night.

You sweep them away as with a flood; they are like a dream, like grass that is renewed in the morning: in the morning it flourishes and is renewed; in the evening it fades and withers.

For we are brought to an end by your anger; by your wrath we are dismayed.

You have set our iniquities before you, our secret sins in the light of your presence.

For all our days pass away under your wrath; we bring our years to an end like a sigh.

The years of our life are seventy, or even by reason of strength eighty; yet their span is but toil and trouble; they are soon gone, and we fly away.

Who considers the power of your anger, and your wrath according to the fear of you?

So teach us to number our days that we may get a heart of wisdom.

Return, O Lord! How long? Have pity on your servants!

Satisfy us in the morning with your steadfast love, that we may rejoice and be glad all our days.

Make us glad for as many days as you have afflicted us, and for as many years as we have seen evil.

Let your work be shown to your servants, and your glorious power to their children.

Let the favor of the Lord our God be upon us, and establish the work of our hands upon us; yes, establish the work of our hands!

The context for Psalm 90 is important, so let's look at it first. The psalm is attributed to Moses, and some biblical scholars suggest that the psalm, or an early version of it, may have been written during the time when the people of Israel were wandering in the wilderness. Other scholars suggest that this version is a reworking of the Mosaic themes and that it was written in the period of the Babylonian exile. Either way, the context of the psalm is clear—the people of God are in a tough spot, their world is full of trouble, and it seems as if God is not at work. Now we are not suffering tremendously in Northwest Arkansas, but we too live in a world full of pain and brokenness. We have had an historical economic downturn that has challenged our sense of security, our plans for the future, and that may bring more crises and hunger to many around the world. We have news reports of a potential pandemic flu virus, of increasing risks of terrorism, of climate change, and of war. In a world full of difficulty, Psalm 90 is a personal prayer, an appeal to God, to give his meaning to our temporary and broken experience of this world. The psalmist begins by recognizing the brevity of life; he then confesses the brokenness of our sin and begs for God to respond, and he affirms his trust in God to build our lives. I don't often use alliteration in my sermons, but today I offer you the four b's of Psalm 90—brevity, brokenness, begging, and building—as my final words to the graduating seniors.

Brevity of life

Psalm 90 begins by acknowledging the brevity of our lives here on earth with metaphor after metaphor: we come from dust and return to dust; we are swept away like a flood; we are like a dream; we are like grass that is green in the morning but that fades and withers by the end of the day; our years end like a sigh. And, when the psalmist suggests that we may live to be seventy or perhaps eighty, he is suggesting a really long life in a time when the average lifespan was closer to fifty. It would be like us saying, we may live to ninety or even a hundred, but even then, the years are soon gone and we fly away.

When I teach literature, I often do an experiment with my class to help them think about the brevity of life, and perhaps you would be willing to join me in that experiment today. If you would, please stand up. Okay, now please stay standing if you know the names of your parents; keep standing if you know the names of your grandparents; keep standing if you know the names of your great grandparents; and your great-great grandparents. What does this experiment prove? It proves that in four generations, it is likely that not even your own family will remember your name—I know, wow, that hurts—but it also gives us a sense of the brevity of our lives.

Do you remember the first time that you knew that you were mortal? That you had a limited amount of time on this earth? That you were going to die? I remember. I was a youngish boy, perhaps ten or twelve, and I had just finished reading in bed and turned out the light. It was late at night, perhaps 11:00 P.M., and there was no moon out that night so my room was dark, jet-black dark. The whole house was quiet, so all I could hear was the hands moving on the cheap clock at the side of my bed—tick, tock, tick, tock, tick, tock. As I lay in bed and listened to the clock, I suddenly realized that every tick of the clock was moving me a second closer to my own death. It was, and still is, a terrifying thought. I immediately turned on the light and unplugged the clock, but I am still reminded of that night when I hear a clock ticking in the dark.

Later in graduate school, I would read Philip Larkin's "Aubade," first published in 1977, which expressed my boyish terror so well. Larkin writes of "unresting death, a whole day nearer now" and "the dread" that accompanies our awareness of death. I expect that you have had similar experiences, that you too have felt the fleetingness of life, particularly on this weekend. Students, you remember as if it were yesterday moving into the residence halls as freshman, meeting your best friend through O-groups or intramurals, the first few days of class when you were trying to figure out what a syllabus was and how you were going to do all this work with four hours of sleep every night. Parents, you remember driving away after dropping off your child that weekend and having to stop at the bank or Sonic or the Taco Bell so that you could stop crying because your sons or daughters were starting to make their transition to adulthood. And now, almost as if it was a dream, tomorrow, you will be graduating from college or watching your sons or daughters graduate from college. Where did the time go?

My wife sometimes thinks that I am too pessimistic, and you might be agreeing with her right now as this sermon does not sound particularly celebratory for a graduation weekend. So, on this day before graduation, why should we reflect on the brevity of our lives? Why should we recognize our mortality? It is because we serve a God who is not mortal, who is not fleeting, who is not ephemeral, who is not transitory. In verse 1, the psalmist tells us that God has been our dwelling place, or in other translations, "our help" in all generations. In verse 2, he tells us that God has been around before the world was created: "before the mountains were brought forth, or ever you had formed the earth and the world, from everlasting to everlasting you are God." Or in verse 4, "a thousand years in your sight are but yesterday when it is past, or a watch in the night." To orient our lives properly, we should come to face our own mortality, and recognize that our only hope is to trust, worship, and follow the one who is not finite or mortal. As Revelation 4 suggests, we will one day pray without ceasing, "Holy, Holy, Holy, is the Lord God almighty, who was, and is, and is to come" (4:8). We can accept the brevity of our lives only because we serve a God who was, and is, and is to come.

Brokenness of life

We also live in a world that is broken. In 1905, *The Times of London* invited several prominent people to respond to the question, "What is wrong with the world?" G. K. Chesterton famously responded with a letter.

> Dear Sirs,
> I am.
> Sincerely yours,
> G. K. Chesterton

Psalm 90 affirms Chesterton's assessment. The psalmist confesses that both collectively and individually we are responsible for the brokenness in the world and that God is not pleased with our sin. In verses 7-8: "For we are brought to an end by your anger; by your wrath we are dismayed. You have set our iniquities before you, our secret sins in the light of your presence."

Do you also remember the first time that you knew that you had done wrong? The first time that you recognized that you sinned? I remember—it was one of my earliest memories. I was probably four or five, and I was sleeping on the couch in the sun porch of my parents' home. My mom called me to come to dinner, and I heard her call me, but, all of sudden, I realized that I could pretend that I didn't hear her. I could pretend that I was still asleep and ignore her call to dinner. In short, I lied and disobeyed. And I am afraid that I found my lie and disobedience to be thrilling because I discovered that I did not have to obey my mother, that I could be in charge of my own life, and that I could get away with it. Sin comes to us naturally and its power is strong, and it is so often about asserting our own will.

We are broken people and we inflict that brokenness on others. Sometimes the brokenness seems petty. We ignore the lonely people because they are different. We ridicule another person to make ourselves feel better. We waste food or time or relationships. We screen our parents' calls, which I think is a sin, because we don't want to be bothered to talk to them. Sometimes the brokenness is more private but still damaging. We spend more than we need to make ourselves feel better. We furtively return to the Web sites that degrade human beings as only sexual. We silently compare ourselves to others and are jealous of their achievements or friendships or status. Sometimes the brokenness is more systemic and more difficult to see. We leave the light on in the room because we are not paying for the electricity and can't see the emissions from the smokestack at the power plant. We live and work and worship in places in which people are just like us, so it is difficult to see the problems or perspectives of others. We avoid people who are struggling without a job or with unplanned pregnancy because we don't know how to help. If our secret thoughts and deeds were uncovered for all to see, it would become clear that we are not much different from the main character in Dostoevsky's *Notes from the Underground*, a character who begins his monologue by saying, "I am a wicked man . . . I am a spiteful man. I am a most unpleasant man."[1]

Begging for God's mercy

Again, however, reflecting on our brokenness should not merely be a masochistic exercise. It should not be just to make ourselves feel bad. The main point of our sin is that it separates us from God. Our reflection should not be primarily about us, but about God, a good God who hates our sin but is yet willing to forgive us. In verse 13 the psalmist begs for God's mercy. "Return, O Lord. How long? Have pity on your servants." The psalmist is asking God to relent from his judgment, to divert his wrath, to turn from the normal consequences of sin and care again for his people. He is asking God to bring them out of exile, and to shower his blessings on them again. Indeed, given the brevity of life and brokenness of the people of God, the psalmist's—and by extension our—only hope for goodness in life is God's mercy and favor, and the psalmist is not shy in asking for it. We too should not be shy in begging for God's forgiveness and mercy, or in encouraging others to recognize their own brokenness and to seek reconciliation with God through Jesus Christ. We believe in that good news, and we should not be shy about sharing it with others.

God's building of our lives

We recognize the brevity of our lives; we recognize our brokenness; and we recognize our need to beg for God's mercy and forgiveness. In that recognition, we begin to see how God builds lasting meaning into our lives. The psalmist asks God to build four things into our lives. In verse 12, the psalmist asks God to "teach us to number our days that we may get a heart of wisdom." Number our days—when I was a lawyer, as part of the firm's billing process, I had to divide each hour into ten units and bill my time in six-minute increments. In other words, if I was on the telephone and talked to a client for six minutes, I would have to write down the name of the client, what I talked about, and then .1, for a tenth of an hour, or six minutes, so that the firm could bill the client for that time. Now if I talked for thirty minutes, I would mark down .5 of an hour. As you might imagine, keeping track of your time in this manner makes you very conscious of how you are spending your time and how efficient you are in using your time. Indeed, Peter Drucker, the founder of the study of management, suggests that any effective executive should periodically do a similar time study to see if they are actually spending time on what is important in their job.

The psalmist not only speaks this truth before my law firm or Peter Drucker, but he also reorients the point of the truth. We know our lives are brief, but we ask God to teach us to number those days—to be conscious of how we are spending our time—so that we can get a heart of wisdom—to gain God's perspective on how to live and be in this world.

And, notice that it is a "heart" of wisdom; it is not just knowing the right thing to do—it is also orienting your whole emotional, physical, intellectual, and spiritual life to follow God's wisdom. God builds lasting value in our lives by teaching us to number our days in order to get a heart of wisdom.

Second, in verse 14, the psalmist asks God, "Satisfy us in the morning with your steadfast love, that we may rejoice and be glad all of our days." Our life in this world is brief and broken, so we can only be satisfied and content in this world when we rely on God's steadfast love, his firmly fixed, resolute, unmoving, undeviatingly constant love that brings joy and gladness.

Third, in verse 16, the psalmist asks God, "Let your work be shown to you servants, and your glorious power to their children." Notice two things here. God reveals his work and his power to his people, and this request is for more than just one generation. The psalmist longs to be a part of God's work, not just for himself and his generation, but for his children and their generation. So, even if our great-great grandchildren may not remember our names, we can still pray that God will remember their names—that his work and power will be shown throughout the generations.

Fourth, in verse 17, the psalmist asks, "Let the favor of the Lord our God be upon us, and establish the work of our hands upon us; yes, establish the work of our hands!" The only way that our work will last will be because it receives God's favor. The psalmist also longs for God to establish his work: he repeats the request twice for emphasis. It is a plea to take our brief and broken lives and make them into something that will last for God's eternity.

And, I think that final plea of the psalmist is particularly apt for us today. Graduating seniors, as you think of your future with anticipation or uncertainty or a mixture of both, I know that many of you long for God to establish the work of your hands. Whether that work is your first job as an engineer or as graduate student in history, in your upcoming marriage or in repairing a relationship with a friend, or in finding a church in which to worship and serve or in taking care of a family member, you long for your life to count for something more. On this day before graduation, I expect that you echo the prayer of the psalmist, "Let the favor of the Lord our God be upon us, and establish the work of our hands upon us; yes, establish the work of our hands!"

Graduating seniors, I would also say that your parents want God to establish the work of their hands, and in many ways, you are the work of their hands. Theirs are the hands that embraced you at birth and fed you when you were unable to feed yourself. Theirs are the hands that taught you to play baseball or to dance ballet, and the hands that opened the books to read with you in bed and the Bible to lead you in church. Theirs are the hands that grabbed your arm before you ran into traffic and grabbed the steering wheel when you were about to hit a curb; theirs are the hands that will give you away in marriage and that will continue to embrace you in life's disappointments. On this day before graduation, I expect your parents echo the prayer of the psalmist, "Let the favor of the Lord our God be upon us, and establish the work of our hands upon us; yes, establish the work of our hands!"

And, I know that JBU's faculty and staff long for God to establish you as the work of our hands. Ours were the hands that wrote your exams and graded your essays; ours were the hands that organized your business-plan competition and directed your voices at the Christmas concert; ours were the hands that were held high to bless you at the end of chapel and that cleaned your bathrooms in the residence halls. Ours were the hands that checked your financial accounts and that demonstrated how to dig a volleyball and ours were the hands that have been clasped in prayer when you were in need and that have applauded you with joy at your accomplishments. You are the work of our collective hands at JBU, and, on this day before graduation, we too echo the prayer of the psalmist, and say, "Let the favor of the Lord our God be upon us, and establish the work of our hands; yes, establish the work of our hands!"

May it always be true of us.

Conclusion: Keeping Track

College represents an intense, life-shaping experience for so many people. Young people head to college ready to leave home but often not quite ready to take on adult life. They are searching to understand their place in the world. Who is God? What am I good at? What should I do for a living? How should I spend my time? Where might I live? Who will be my friends? Whom might I marry, if at all? In the liberal-arts context, they are also coming to grips with some of the greatest minds and ideas of human history, and are seeking to understand how those ideas shape their response to contemporary culture. They also often question authority, whether it be their friends, parents, faculty, the church, and even God. Yet they also long to find answers that will orient their lives with meaning, answers that they often find from their friends, parents, faculty, the church, and God. Moreover, the living and learning context of the residential college enables these conversations to spill over from the classroom to the cafeteria, from the dorm room to the service project. The intensity of this life-learning experience carves deep patterns of being in emerging adults.

It is a wonderful gift to spend your career working with students during such an intensive, formative time in their lives, but the questions that they face are not unique. We face them again and again as adults, albeit with different nuances and with different levels of intensity. We still have times of faith and of doubt; we still need to be more grateful or kind; we still fear failure or disappointment; we still live in exile and need to be diligent in our ordinary obedience. In other words, we still need to hear God's Word speak in our lives. I trust that God has spoken his words of correction, instruction, and encouragement to you through the words of this book.

And, while it is a great joy to work with young people in a university setting, there is also annual sorrow to the rhythm of the academic life. At the end of each year, you say goodbye to seniors whom you have watched grow and mature into adults with such promise. You say goodbye right about the time that you could imagine them being peers, even friends. You say goodbye just as you begin to see the return on the investment in their lives. So the celebration of graduation is always tinged with the wistful sadness of separation, both for students and for faculty and staff.

Of course, this pattern too is repeated throughout our adult lives. We form bonds of friendship at work or in church or in the community, but then new opportunities lead the work colleague away, or a close family leaves the church for a new ministry, or the neighbor passes away from illness, and the loss of friendship is felt keenly. Indeed, as a lifelong reader and English professor, I often have a similar sense of loss when I finish a book. The book enables a friendship of sorts to develop between reader and writer, a relationship that is both personal and distant at the same time in that the writer shares intimate details of his or her interior life with people whom he or she knows little about. Speaking in chapel to over a thousand students offers a similar sense of distant intimacy, and I have found that Gerard Manley Hopkins' "The Lantern Out of Doors," offers me the best way to say goodbye to graduating seniors. I read the poem at the end of each of my baccalaureate addresses, and it seems an apt way to conclude this book.

In the poem, the speaker is looking at the light of a lantern as a person carries it across the horizon. He is following that light with his eye and wonders about the life of the person who is carrying the lantern.

> Sometimes a lantern moves along the night,
> That interests our eyes. And who goes there?
> I think; where from and bound, I wonder, where,
> With, all down darkness wide, his wading light?

> Men go by me, whom either beauty bright
> In mould or mind or what not else makes rare:
> They rain against our much-thick and marsh air
> Rich beams, till death or distance buys them quite.

We all have the privilege of watching how people's unique gifts and talents burn "beauty bright" and make them rare. However, like the speaker in the poem, we are all limited in our human attention, and we soon lose sight of those we knew.

> Death or distance soon consumes them: wind,
> What most I may eye after, be in at the end
> I cannot, and out of sight is out of mind.

Out of sight is out of mind. It is one of the great sorrows of our human condition that we say goodbye to friends, that we lose track of those to whom we were close, that despite our best intentions we cannot keep in touch with everyone. "I cannot, and out of sight is out of mind." Ah, but then Hopkins gives us an answer for this sorrow.

> Christ minds: Christ's interest, what to avow or amend,
> There, eyes them, heart wants, care haunts, foot follows kind
> Their ransom, their rescue, and first, fast, last friend.

We cannot keep track of each other, but Christ can. We are limited, but Christ is sufficient. We are broken, but Christ is whole. So, we can say good-bye to others with hope because we commit them to Christ, the only one who can continue to watch our lanterns, the only one who can bring about our ransom and our rescue, the only one who can be our "first, fast, last friend."

May it also be true of us who follow Jesus Christ.

Endnotes

Introduction: Chapel in the University

1. George Marsden, *The Soul of the American University: From Protestant Establishment to Established Nonbelief* (New York: Oxford University Press, 1994), 4, 5.
2. Marsden, 345.
3. Duane Litfin, *Conceiving the Christian College* (Grand Rapids: Wm. B. Eerdmans, 2004), 261.

Chapter 1: Opening the Year: Who Are We? Living in Community

1. Frederick Buechner, *The Final Beast* (New York: Harper Collins, 1982), 175.
2. Ernest Gordon, *To End All Wars* (Grand Rapids: Zondervan, 2002), 73.
3. Gordon, 223-4.
4. C. S. Lewis, *Mere Christianity* (New York: Touchstone, 1980), 11.

Chapter 2: First Semester: Who Am I? Beloved Child of God

1. Timothy Keller, *Reason for God: Belief in the Age of Skepticism* (New York: Dutton, 2008), 206.

Chapter 4: Second Semester: What Am I to Do? Vocation

1. Frederick Buechner, *Wishful Thinking: A Seeker's ABC* (New York: HarperOne, 1993), 118.

Chapter 5: The Baccalaureate Service: Saying Farewell

1. Fyodor Dostoevsky, *Notes from the Underground* (New York: Vintage, 1993), vii.